Florence and Tuscany Travel Guide

Book 1

A DETAILED GUIDE TO FLORENCE AND PISTOIA

Florence: The living embodiment of art

George Esperidis

Florence: The mother of cities

Everything you need to see, hear, and, of course, taste

A few words from the author

If you are holding this book, you are probably a seasoned traveler who takes a thorough approach to planning your trip. You seek not only vibrant experiences but also new and intriguing knowledge. This guide is exactly what you need!

My name is George Esperidis. I am an art historian, traveler, and passionate admirer of Italy. With the help of my guide, "Florence—the Living Embodiment of Art," we will embark on a journey through Florence—one of the most beautiful cities in Europe, a pivotal center of the Renaissance, and a trendsetter in cultural fashion. In addition, through my guide, "All Shades of Tuscany," we will travel through Tuscany—the land of wine, cheese, and architectural masterpieces.

On our captivating journey spanning 22 centuries, we will visit the homes of Dante and the powerful Medici family, as well as discover what true Tuscans eat. In addition to fascinating stories about Florence and the towns of Tuscany, my guide offers:

1. The best cafés, restaurants, taverns, and bars (with the latest information available).
2. Useful tips on choosing neighborhoods for accommodation so that nothing disrupts your ability to enjoy Florence and Tuscany to the fullest!
3. Advice on purchasing transportation tickets and other essential details that other guides often overlook!

In this guide, I present a program for a walking tour of Florence, as well as an introduction to the main attractions of the city close to the Tuscan capital—Pistoia. Note that my program does not account for the time required to visit all the museums, as this is a matter of personal preference. For example, some might be interested only in the Uffizi Gallery, where one can "get lost" for a whole week if not for the persistent security guards ushering everyone out at closing time. Others might wish to enjoy several museums but view only the main exhibits. Therefore, I focus only on the most significant collections and exhibits of certain museums. In that way, I leave the planning of museum visits to my readers.

All the information in this guide is reliable and meant to entertain.

Thank you for reading this book, and I wish you a pleasant holiday in the heart of Italy!

Sincerely yours,

George Esperides

Table of Contents

1

When are the best times to visit Tuscany and Florence?

The best times to travel are typically spring (from April to the end of May) and autumn (from October to mid or late November). During these periods, Florence (as well as other cities in Tuscany) sees fewer tourists, so you won't have to endure long queues to enter city museums or wait endlessly for a table at a restaurant. Additionally, spring and autumn in Tuscany offer the most pleasant weather: The heat has either yet to arrive or begun to wane, which makes walks along the stone-paved streets of the region's ancient cities less exhausting. You also won't need to constantly carry an umbrella, as Tuscany experiences heavy rains in winter.

In spring, all of Tuscany is adorned with the lush bloom of the most fragrant herbs and plants, transforming its already enchanting landscapes into something truly extraordinary. However, if you are allergic to flower pollen, then autumn would be the ideal time for you to explore this land of wine, meat, and architectural masterpieces.

2

What are important considerations before traveling?

The most important part of any journey is planning and organization. Tuscany is a favorite destination for tourists, and insufficient attention to early booking of hotels, tickets, or car rentals can ruin your vacation. Of course, we won't allow this to happen.

Even if you plan to travel in autumn or spring—before the official tourist season begins or after it ends—it is worth booking tickets to the main museums of Florence and renting a car in advance for trips to Pisa, Lucca, and other wonderful Tuscan cities.

Tickets and tours to most of Florence's most popular museums—the Uffizi Gallery, the Accademia Gallery, the Palatine Gallery, and so on—can be booked online on the Italy Museum website in the Florence section. (Later in the book, I will discuss the main museums of Florence in detail.) On this same website, you can find a hotel if you do not want to rent an apartment on a daily basis.

If you plan to rent a car, keep in mind that certain parts of Tuscan cities have traffic restrictions. These areas are marked as "zona a Traffico Limitato" (ZTL). In Florence, for example, Piazza del Duomo, Via Tornabuoni, and Piazza Pitti are entirely pedestrian zones. Entering these squares and streets by vehicle (except for taxis, fire trucks, and ambulances) is subject to a hefty fine.

3

Introduction

A few words about Tuscany: The country of meat, wine, and architectural masterpieces

Perhaps it was here that ancient Roman culture truly began: in this picturesque, hilly region washed by the waters of the Tyrrhenian Sea. To be more precise, it wasn't exactly ancient Roman culture but, rather, Etruscan culture—the very foundation upon which the better-known ancient Roman culture would arise. The origins of the Etruscans remain a mystery to this day, but their civilization was certainly quite advanced. The future ancient Romans inherited from the Etruscans the arts of gladiatorial combat, chariot racing, and funeral rites. As mentioned in the brief history of Florence, the memory of the Etruscans is preserved in local place names: "Tuscany" is derived from the Latin "Tuscia"—the "land of the Etruscans," as the ancient Romans referred to their predecessors in these lands. The Tyrrhenian Sea is also named in honor of this enigmatic people: The Etruscans were called "Tyrrhenians" or "Tyrrhenes" by the ancient Greeks.

Today, Tuscany is inhabited by Tuscans—yes, the residents primarily consider themselves Tuscans, Florentines, Pisans, and so on. Only collectively do they refer to themselves as Italians. In Italy, as in the United Kingdom, a multitude of small states existed for a long time on a relatively small territory. These states united into a single nation just 160 years ago, in 1861. Over the centuries preceding this date, during which the Apennine Peninsula was divided by numerous state borders, a wide variety of Italian dialects developed: Tuscan (which became the basis of the literary Italian language), Venetian, Neapolitan, Sicilian, and many others. These dialects still exist and play an important role in forming the national identity of the inhabitants of various regions of Italy. Yes, in reality, it is a bit more complex than just pizza, pasta, and Chianti.

Tuscany spans an area of 22,994 square kilometers (8,878 square miles) and is home to about 3.7 million people. This region is one of the largest wine-producing centers in Europe, with a centuries-old family tradition of winemaking: The Antinori and Frescobaldi houses have been producing their wines for the past 700 years. Incidentally, the pioneers of winemaking in Tuscany were likely the Etruscans. The amphorae, in which local wines were exported to the southern peninsula, date back to the 8th and 7th centuries BC.

As the birthplace of the Italian Renaissance, Tuscany is renowned for its "cities of art": Florence, Siena, Lucca, Arezzo, Pisa, and San Gimignano. Three major schools of painting—Lucchese, Sienese, and Florentine—originated and thrived in Tuscany. It is here that great masters such as Leonardo da Vinci, Michelangelo Buonarroti,

4

Dante Alighieri, Giotto di Bondone, and many others were born, grew up, and achieved immortal fame.

But Signora Tuscany can tempt you with more than spiritual nourishment. The local cuisine is intriguing and distinctive. One famous dish is bistecca alla fiorentina. This is a Florentine steak made from the loin of a young steer or heifer, traditionally served with cannellini beans, olive oil, and a cabbage salad and accompanied by a glass of Chianti Classico—arguably the most famous of Tuscan red wines. Another renowned dish is the peasant soup ribollita, made from bread, beans, carrots, Tuscan lacinato kale, onions, potatoes, and sometimes beets. The word "ribollita" means "reboiled" or "cooked twice," and the name pays tribute to the fact that peasants typically made it in large quantities on Fridays, then reheated it in deep pans over the following days, "reboiling" it to the consistency of a thick porridge. Also quite famous is the Florentine sausage salami finocchiona. It is distinguished from regular salami mainly by the use of fennel instead of pepper in its preparation.

Another well-known Tuscan appetizer is the classic "Crostini neri" or "Black Crostini," which are small pieces of bread spread with a special pâté made from chicken liver, onions, Tuscan olive oil, celery or carrots (depending on the location and the chef's preference), anchovies, and capers. This recipe is predominantly found in Florence, Pistoia, Arezzo, and Prato. Another dish that I strongly recommend is "peposo all'imprunetina"—select Tuscan beef cooked in a clay pot with black peppercorns, garlic, Chianti wine, and salt. The meat is simmered for three hours until it resembles a pâté and is served with fresh Tuscan bread, onto which it is traditionally spread. According to tradition, "peposo all'imprunetina" was invented by the great Florentine architect Filippo Brunelleschi. He is said to have fed this dish to his workers while they were building the dome of the Cathedral of Santa Maria del Fiore. In a way, this dish is the most Florentine of any you can find in Tuscany.

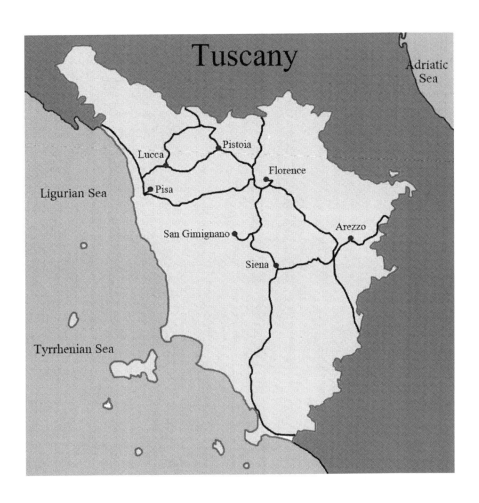

4

A brief history of Florence:
The city of eternal Renaissance

Once, on the banks of the Arno River, the eternal forces of good and evil merged to create a city of astonishing contradictions, where bloody tyrants donated millions to the creation of the greatest works of art, where the Renaissance, the son of great antiquity, took its first breath, and where time itself retreated, halting its relentless grind. This city is Florence.

Strolling—no, not strolling but slowly drifting through these ancient streets between churches and palazzos, from square to square, among the stones bathed in gentle sunlight the color of fresh bread crust, it might seem as though this city has always been here. But, of course, that is not the case, at least not on a cosmic scale. The founding of Florence is usually dated to 59 BC, and the circumstances of this event are ambiguous. According to some accounts, the city began life as a village for military veterans. During the late Roman Republic, when army service became the domain of professionals rather than conscripts, all who completed their term received a plot of land, a pension, Roman citizenship, and freedom from all obligations. According to other accounts, the famous Gaius Julius Caesar ordered the construction of Florence as an outpost to counter the garrison of the rebellious Lucius Sergius Catilina. The garrison was located six kilometers (3.12 miles) from this spot, and Lucius Sergius Catilina was attempting to seize consular power in the Republic by military means. What can be stated with certainty is that the founding of Florence was closely tied to the military, as many years later, having become a full-fledged Roman city, it was officially dedicated to the god of war, Mars.

There is no consensus on the origin of the city's name, either. According to the poetic version, the name indicates the time of the city's founding, which fell on the "Floralia"—festivals that were dedicated to the ancient Roman goddess of spring, Flora, and that were held annually from April 28 to May 3. According to the logical version, "Florence" is simply a modification of the Latin word "Fluentia," literally meaning "flow," thus pointing to the city's location at the confluence of the Arno and Mugnone Rivers. I don't know about you, but I much prefer the first theory.

Either way, the first reliable information about the life of the settlement dates back only to 123 AD, when the first stone bridge over the Arno River was built. By that time, Florence had all the essential attributes of a Roman city: baths, aqueducts, a forum, an amphitheater, and, of course, a river port, which facilitated trade with Pisa.

By the end of the 3rd century AD, the city had become an important center. Here, Emperor Diocletian stationed the headquarters of a legion commander responsible for the entire region of Tuscia, which is known today as Tuscany. This name derives from the Etruscans—the ancient people who inhabited these lands before the arrival of the

Latins. The origin of the Etruscans remains a subject of debate. However, it is known that the Latins adopted, from them, many things that we associate with Ancient Rome: the art of gladiatorial combat and chariot racing. The toponym "Etruria," directly pointing to the ancient inhabitants of these lands, will appear again on our journey, so I advise you, my dear companion, to keep it in mind.

At the very beginning of the 4th century, merchants from the East (Greece and Syria) brought Christianity to Florence. This religion was later fused with ancient art to produce the countless masterpieces of the Italian Renaissance. Upon Christianity's arrival, the city was already an important trading center on the Apennine Peninsula, with a population of about 15,000 people. (The capital of the empire, Rome, had about 750,000 inhabitants.) The first Christian church in Florence appeared at that time, outside the city's fortress walls, and in 313 AD, the first Florentine bishop—Felix (translated from Latin as "Happy")—was mentioned.

It seems that the new religious teaching spread rather slowly among the city's inhabitants. The decisive event in the "Christianization" of Florence was the invasion by Germanic barbarian Ostrogoths led by Radagaisus (not to be confused with Radagast the Brown from "The Hobbit," who has nothing to do with this) in 405-406 AD. The main roles in the defense of the Florentine fortress were played by Emperor Honorius's general, Flavius Stilicho (himself a former Vandal), who brought 15,000 soldiers from Liguria, and the Christian bishop Zenobius, who gathered the townspeople for a large prayer service. Florence's salvation from Radagaisus's Ostrogoths was attributed to Zenobius's prayers rather than Stilicho's military skills. It is believed that this event led the few remaining pagan inhabitants, "struck by the power of the Christian God," to convert, thus making Florence a wholly Christian city. Mars was deposed as the city's patron deity and replaced by John the Baptist (though this might have occurred somewhat later). One of the city's first churches, Santa Reparata, was erected and dedicated to the early Christian martyr Reparata of Caesarea, whose memory was celebrated on the day of the Ostrogoths' repulsion from Florence. She, alongside John the Baptist, became one of the city's heavenly patrons. Today, the famous cathedral of Santa

Maria del Fiore stands on the site of Santa Reparata. However, remnants of the ancient church, including a beautiful mosaic floor, can still be seen in the areas beneath Florence's main architectural masterpiece.

Dark times came for Florence, as for all of Italy, after 476 AD, when the commander of the Roman mercenary army, Odoacer, forced the last Western Roman Emperor, Romulus Augustulus, to abdicate and declared himself the first King of Italy and viceroy of the Eastern Roman Emperor Zeno. The unified Roman Empire had been divided into Western and Eastern Empires in 395 AD, after the death of Emperor Theodosius I. While no radical changes occurred in the lives of the Romans under Odoacer's rule (contrary to the common belief in the "catastrophe of Ancient Rome," old institutions of power were preserved, and relative peace and prosperity reigned after 473 AD), Florence was ravaged in the mid-6th century during the so-called "Gothic Wars." These wars were sparked by the Eastern Roman Empire's (Byzantium's) attempt to reclaim control over the lands of Italy. At the time, these lands were held by the rebellious Ostrogoths, whose main territories were located here in Tuscany. The wars lasted about 20 years, during which time Florence was captured by the Byzantines (541 AD), reclaimed and burned by the Ostrogoths (550 AD), and recaptured by the Greeks in the same year. According to Byzantine sources, the army of Greek general Narses found the city destroyed and depopulated after the Ostrogoths, but archaeological evidence does not confirm these accounts. Moreover, many researchers consider a beautifully preserved structure from that period, the Torre della Pagliazza on Piazza Sant'Elisabetta, to be the oldest building in the city, having remained intact since its construction. We will discuss this in more detail later.

However, after defeating the Ostrogoths, the Greeks could not hold Italy for long. In 568, another Germanic tribe, the Lombards (yes, the Germans didn't let Italy live in peace), invaded the northeastern part of Italy. Under their rule, Florence fell into complete decline, as the new rulers took control of the crucial trade routes connecting Florence with nearby cities like Altopascio and Fucecchio and, most importantly, Rome. Due to the decline in trade and, consequently, in production, this period became the true "dark ages" for Florence. Ancient manuscripts often linked the "revival" of Florence to the legendary unifier of the West, Charlemagne, who stayed in the city in 781 and 786 after the Franks (oddly enough, also of Germanic origin) conquered the Lombard Kingdom of Italy. Indeed, during Charlemagne's time, Florence experienced some changes, and the memory of his presence at the laying of the first stone of the future church of Santi Apostoli is preserved in a marble plaque in front of it. However, the city truly flourished only under Charlemagne's grandson, Lothair I, in 825-854. During his reign, the Imperial School of Rhetoric, Law, and Liberal Arts was established in Florence, and the city became the capital of a province (county) within the Kingdom of Italy.

NICOLAVS·II·PP·BVRGVNDIO·

Pope Nicolas II

The true golden age of Florence came in the 11th century and laid a strong foundation for the city's future transformation into one of the capitals of the Italian Renaissance. At that time, Tuscany, as well as Modena, Ferrara, Mantua, Brescia, and Reggio (almost all of northern Italy), were ruled by the House of Canossa, a family of Lombard origin. During the reign of the Margraves from the House of Canossa, a Florentine bishop, Gerard of Burgundy, was elected Pope for the first time, taking the name Nicholas II. (Yes, in those days, ruling houses could and did influence the election of a pope).

The Margraves of Canossa, who controlled almost all of northern Italy, played a key role in the late 11th-century conflict between the Holy Roman Emperors and the Roman Popes for supreme power in the empire. One manifestation of this conflict was the right to appoint abbots and bishops in the imperial principalities. This was known as the right of investiture, and it gave the conflict its name—the "Investiture Controversy." The last representative of the House of Canossa, Margravine Matilda, played a crucial role in the struggle between Pope Gregory VII and Emperor Henry IV. She lived in Florence with her large personal guard, ensuring relative peace in the city during those turbulent times when half of its inhabitants supported the pontiff

and the other half the monarch. The coat of arms of the House of Canossa depicted a dog standing on its hind legs, gnawing a bone, and the family's motto read, "When the dog finishes the bone, the House of Canossa will end." The dog finished the bone on July 24, 1115, when Margravine Matilda died. Having no heirs, she bequeathed her vast possessions to the Catholic Church.

Matilda of Tuscany

These holdings, of course, included Florence. Following this "transfer of ownership," the city found itself effectively without direct governance, as the Catholic Church at that time had priorities other than managing Florence. This situation spurred the Florentines to establish local self-government, leading to the formation of the future Florentine Republic. Just ten years after Margravine Matilda's death, the city was first documented as having consuls at its head: Burellus, Florenzitus, Broccardus, and Servolus. It is also likely that a council known as "Bonomini" or "Good Men" was established. It consisted of 150 members elected four times a year by the citizens of Florence, and consuls were accountable to it.

During this period in the mid-12th century, the political scene saw the emergence of families destined to make their names legendary through their patronage of the artists, sculptors, and architects of the Renaissance: the Buondelmonti, Gherardini, Scolari, Strozzi, and Brunelleschi families, among many others.

Soon, the wealthiest and most influential families of Florence began to form alliances—"coteries"—that effectively took over the city's governance in the latter half of the 12th century. Naturally, the rivalry among these "coteries" led to a brief but bloody civil war. This conflict became the catalyst for the abolition of the consul system, which proved ineffective when several powerful families sought to eliminate each other. In place of the consuls, the citizens established the position of "podestà," an elected city manager chosen by the city council. The podestà had to be from another city (to avoid local familial influences), possess knightly rank, and have expertise in law and military affairs. This effectively limited candidates to the nobility. The podestà was responsible for representing supreme authority in diplomatic, civil, and judicial matters, though real power remained with the city's oligarchic council.

By the early 13th century, the old noble families had to share power with new families of wealthy merchants and craftsmen. They formed a new class of urban elite that played a significant role in city governance. This strengthening of the mercantile and artisan classes likely contributed to the swift economic prosperity of the Florentine

Republic. By the 1170s, it had only taken three years to construct a new city wall—indicating not only Florence's wealth but also its level of technical advancement.

Note the elegant twist in history before the Renaissance begins to dawn: Just like in ancient Athens, monarchy disappears in Florence, and power first passes to a limited group of oligarchs. Then, after a long struggle among the classes, it "flows" to the majority of Florentine citizens, giving birth to democracy or, in Latin terms, a republic. Thus, Florence becomes a second ancient Athens. It is not surprising that this city would become the center of the Renaissance, just as Athens was the center of ancient culture, for art thrives on freedom.

This period of freedom, known in the city's history as the "People's Government," began in the mid-13th century after the Florentines expelled the imperial vicar Frederick of Antioch and the families supporting him, who had established the German Emperor's complete control over Florence shortly before. After expelling the vicar, the citizens created a new system of governance. Alongside the podestà and his two assisting consuls, they introduced the post of "captain of the people." This position, countering the podestà who represented the nobility's interests, advocated for the "middle class"—the craftsmen and merchants organized into "guilds," a prototype of unions. This new system proved so effective that within two years of its establishment, Florence was one of the fastest-growing Italian cities and had introduced its gold coin, the florin, which would become the principal currency in Mediterranean trade.

Of course, perpetual peace was slow to arrive in the city: Clashes between supporters of the Roman Popes and the Holy Roman Emperors prevented Florence from enjoying tranquility for a long time. For example, the conflict between the radical Guelphs (uncompromising supporters of the pope, known as "Black Guelphs") and the "liberal" ("White") Guelphs, who were willing to ally with the Ghibellines—the supporters of the Emperor—resulted in the exile of the great Dante and the father of Francesco Petrarch. They, along with other "White Guelphs," were expelled from Florence when the "Blacks" seized power in the city in 1302.

However, political strife did not hinder the city's prosperity. Shortly before the expulsion of Dante and the "White Guelphs" from Florence, construction began on the Cathedral of Santa Maria del Fiore. More precisely, the preparatory work started: The ancient church of Santa Reparata, which had become hopelessly dilapidated, was dismantled down to its foundation to make way for a new cathedral. This cathedral was intended to surpass even Constantinople's Hagia Sophia, which at that time was the largest Christian church in the world. It would be dedicated to the "Holy Virgin Mary with the Flower of the Lily" ("Fiore" referring to the iris flower or "Heraldic Lily," symbolizing the Immaculate Conception and the emblem of Florence).

The 1347 outbreak of the plague, which claimed the lives of about 60% of Europe's population within five years, had a profound impact on Renaissance art. In Florence, from March to October 1348, about 96,000 of the 120,000 living in the city before the epidemic died from the plague. During this time, the future "fathers of the Renaissance" began to ponder the possibility that God had abandoned humanity, as even the Papal Curia could not find an explanation for such a horrific catastrophe. This led to the rise of humanism, a philosophy declaring that the purpose of human existence might lie not only in the worship and understanding of God but also in the improvement and knowledge of oneself, for unlike humans, God is infinite.

Boccaccio's "The Plague of Florence in 1348,"
Etching by L. Sabatelli, late 18th century.

One of the victims of the plague in Avignon (a city in the south of France) was Laure de Noves, the beloved of the Florentine Francesco Petrarch. Petrarch celebrated her memory for ten years in his sonnets, which comprised one of the most significant collections in the history of Italian literature, "Il Canzoniere."

Another victim of the epidemic was the sculptor Andrea Pisano, who, along with Giotto, worked on the decoration of the famous campanile of the Cathedral of Santa Maria del Fiore. Giotto himself died eleven years before the epidemic, having completed only the first tier of his famous campanile, which was finally finished in the early 15th century.

Petrarch's Laura, after Giorgione.

In the late 13th century, specifically in 1292, extremely important reforms were carried out in the Florentine Republic. This led to the formation of the "Second Democracy" and the complete removal of the hereditary aristocracy from the city's governance. The author of these reforms was Giano della Bella, a member of the wool merchants' guild. Della Bella was perhaps one of the first to realize that power lay not with those of noble birth but with those who were wealthier. During this period, the office of the "Gonfalonier of Justice" was established. Gonfaloniers were city standard-bearers (named after the rectangular banner called a gonfalon). The Gonfalonier headed the Signoria (Priory), or the city government, which included representatives from the craft guilds. The Gonfalonier was chosen by lot from among the members of Florence's senior guilds and served for a term of only two months. This short term balanced the broad powers (legislative initiative, military command, convening councils) he held and helped prevent new attempts at power usurpation in the Republic.

Ironically, it was through the position of Gonfalonier that the Medici family came to power. This banking family, which rose by issuing loans to ruling houses and later to royal dynasties, eventually intermarried with the Habsburgs and Bourbons and managed to ascend to the Papal Throne (with Medici Popes Leo X, Pius IV, Clement VII, and Leo XI). In 1530, following their expulsion from Florence, the Medici, with the support of Emperor Charles V, captured the city after a ten-month siege. Then, the last Gonfalonier of Justice, Alessandro de' Medici, was proclaimed the first Duke of Florence.

The Medici tyranny, marked by the excesses of the Inquisition and the transformation of Florence into the capital of the Grand Duchy of Tuscany, lasted 173 years. Despite the despotic rule of the dukes, their capital remained one of Europe's most important cultural centers. In the late 16th century, the first operas in history were staged at the court of the renowned patron of musicians, Grand Duke Ferdinando I.

Ferdinando I de' Medici

The relative liberalization in Florence's life, which by then bore little resemblance to its former republican governance, did not occur until the early 18th century under the rule of Grand Duke Gian Gastone. Ironically, under his reign, the Medici lineage came to an end. After his death, Florence, along with all of Tuscany, was transferred to Francis III, former Duke of Lorraine, who renounced his rights to Lorraine upon marrying Archduchess Maria Theresa, the only daughter and heir of Emperor Charles VI of Austria. In those times, states were considered the private property of ruling houses, and no one bothered to ask the Florentines for their opinion on the "transfer" of their country to another ruler. Marriage to the heir to the Austrian throne required Francis III to renounce the Lorrainian throne and cede his country to France (again, without consulting the inhabitants of Lorraine). The Grand Duchy of Tuscany, in terms of area and value, seemed a fair exchange for Lorraine, especially because the Medici dynasty had conveniently ended.

Thus, the Habsburg-Lorraine house ruled Tuscany until the unification of Italy in 1860-1861, with a brief interruption during the Napoleonic Wars: In 1801, after the annexation by France of several small duchies and principalities in Northern Italy previously belonging to the Bourbons, Napoleon Bonaparte "gifted" them the Grand Duchy of Tuscany as "compensation" for their recent losses and transformed Florence into the capital of the Kingdom of Etruria (again, without consulting the Florentines). Etruria lasted only a short time;

The first King of Italy,
Vittorio Emanuele II.
Photo portrait from 1861

by 1807, it had been annexed by the French Empire, and in 1815, the Habsburgs returned to Tuscany.

The revolutionary wave of 1848, which swept through all of Europe, shook Italy and became its first major step toward unifying the many small duchies, principalities, and kingdoms into a single country. In Florence, as well as in Modena and Venice, where power was in the hands of the Austrian Habsburg-Lorraine house, revolutionary sentiments were especially strong and expressed primarily in hatred of the Austrian rulers, who firmly upheld medieval traditions. For the Grand Duke of Tuscany, Leopold II, the 1848 revolution resulted in a temporary loss of power, which he managed to restore only by "granting" a constitution and convening a parliament. However, by 1852, Leopold had repealed his constitution and concluded a concordat with the Papal Throne, granting the Catholic clergy extraordinarily broad powers in his country (a move that many Florentines opposed). Ultimately, Leopold II was forced to abdicate in 1859 when a mass uprising erupted in Florence. This led to the complete and final overthrow of the Habsburgs in Tuscany and the incorporation of the central part of the Apennine Peninsula into the Kingdom of Italy in 1861.

Shortly after, in 1864, the first King of Italy, Victor Emmanuel II, ordered the transfer of the country's capital from Turin to Florence. Rome would not become the capital of Italy until 1871, when the Papal State, of which Rome was the capital, was abolished. The transfer of the capital was driven by the fact that Turin was dangerously close to the border with France and Austria, where a new war was brewing. To ensure Florence was capable of accepting the status of the government center of the new state, architect Giuseppe Poggi was commissioned to expand the city. Between 1865 and 1871, under his guidance, the ancient walls of Florence were demolished. In their place, ring boulevards inspired by the contemporary reconstruction of Paris by Baron Haussmann were created, culminating in Piazzale Michelangelo. Additionally, a gasometer was installed in Florence to regulate the pressure of "city gas" that lit the streets. Thanks to a state loan project that raised about 30 million Italian lire, Poggi's project was realized in five years. However, the transfer of the capital from Florence to Rome immediately after the annexation of the Papal State in 1871 halted the city's development.

Despite everything, the 19th century brought a new "renaissance" to Florence—both economically and socially. The city's population doubled after 1861, and even the May 18, 1895 earthquake, which significantly damaged city monuments, did not hinder Florence's rapid recovery. The city became an unofficial capital of European culture, attracting young artists, sculptors, writers, and patrons from all over Europe. In 1907, the French Institute of Florence was established. It was followed by the British Institute in 1917. Both continue to study Franco-Italian and Anglo-Italian cultural relations, respectively.

After Mussolini's overthrow in 1943, Florence was occupied by German troops who carried out mass executions of members of the Italian anti-fascist resistance and sympathetic Florentines. The city remained under Nazi control until August 1944, when it was liberated through fierce battles involving an uprising within Florence and the advance of the 2nd New Zealand Division into Tuscany. Many of its neighborhoods were destroyed, but they were meticulously restored in the following years.

Today, Florence remains as significant a cultural and economic center of Italy as it was centuries ago. The city's importance to European and world culture is immeasurable, and it attracts art enthusiasts and tourists from around the globe. And now, my dear traveler, we shall no longer delay our own exhilarating rendezvous with her—the magnificent lily of the Apennines, the one and only Florence.

Odoardo Borrani. "Rendezvous in the Uffizi," 1878.

5

Florence: Long-awaited date

Piazza della Signoria

Yes, this is it—the famous Piazza della Signoria, the starting point for the history of Florence and all of Tuscany. The oldest and still the most important square in the city, it was the center of settlement even in Roman times when a theater, baths, and a textile dyeing workshop were established there. (The lineage of the renowned Florentine manufactories of the Renaissance traces back to these establishments.) If you step into this square early on a weekday morning, especially in spring or mid-autumn, when the sun has just risen above the horizon and has not yet gently tickled the black nose of the brave Marzocco, firmly holding the Florentine lily at the Palazzo Vecchio, you will feel as if time has frozen around you. Do not hurry; let this time embrace you, surround you, and immerse you in itself.

You will hear the echoes of 1497 when a bonfire was lit in this square. It is known as the "Bonfire of the Vanities," and in it, luxurious dresses, mirrors in splendid frames, non-theological books, dice, and playing cards were burned. Botticelli himself threw two of his paintings into the flames. All these items were confiscated from the Florentines by order of Girolamo Savonarola, a church reformer and unyielding opponent of Pope Alexander VI (the infamous Borgia) and the Medici clan, which already ruled Tuscany at that time. Savonarola, coming from an old Paduan family, was known from childhood for his piety and Christian virtue, as well as his inclination toward asceticism. The latter fully manifested in him after an unhappy love affair with a girl from the Florentine Strozzi family. Having become completely disillusioned with worldly life, Girolamo entered a monastery and dedicated himself to fighting the excesses and sins in which the Catholic Church was mired at that time.

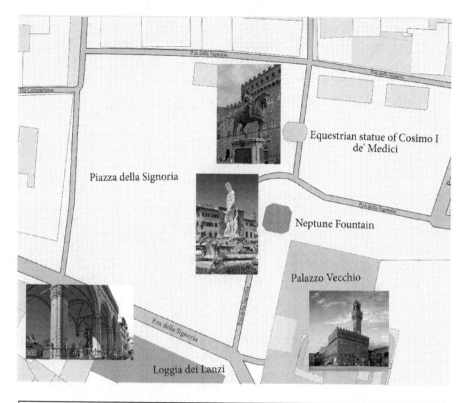

Piazza della Signoria

Equestrian statue of Cosimo I
de' Medici

Neptune Fountain

Palazzo Vecchio

Loggia dei Lanzi

Map of Piazza della Signoria

Savonarola condemned Pope Alexander VI for his excessive nepotism (Borgia granted cardinalships and noble titles to all his relatives and friends) and for the moral decay at his court in Rome (the dominance of courtesans and the pope's alleged cohabitation with his own daughter). The ruler of Florence and the Tuscan aristocrats were chastised for their "pagan humanism" and "total depravity," as the Florentines allowed themselves to read and analyze ancient pagan philosophers instead of the Bible and theological texts, thereby placing man above God.

Ultimately, Savonarola became the de facto ruler of Florence when the French King Charles VIII's troops entered Tuscany and expelled Piero di Lorenzo de' Medici, who had inherited power in the republic from his father, Lorenzo the Magnificent. It was then that the radical republican Girolamo Savonarola initiated the "purge of luxury": "The rich appropriate the wages of the common people, all income, and taxes," he said. "Any excess is a mortal sin, as it costs the lives of the poor."

Savonarola first reformed Florence's tax system, which, under the Medici, was, to put it bluntly, quite unfair, and established a maximum income tax rate of 10%. The preacher

Girolamo Savonarola

then proclaimed Jesus Christ as the "lord and king of Florence" and himself as His chosen one. In his addresses to the people, delivered in this very square, Savonarola called for the burning of sodomites at the stake, the cutting out of the tongues of blasphemers, the singing of only psalms, and the reading of only the Bible.

Of course, historical records do not confirm such widespread repressions in Florence during Savonarola's "dictatorship." (Only one person was burned at the stake on charges of sodomy, and most punishments were fines or whippings.) However, it is clear that he managed to instill fear in the inhabitants, as within a few months of his rise to power, all songs ceased, and carnivals were no longer held in the city.

Eventually, the French left Florence, and Pope Alexander VI (as was expected) excommunicated Savonarola. He also threatened to excommunicate all of Florence and anyone "who would listen to the mad preacher or speak with him." Despite this, the Republic's government hesitated to act against Savonarola, who, in response to his excommunication, called for a General Council to depose the pope. However, his letter with this appeal, sent to King Charles VIII of France (at that time one of the most powerful monarchs in Europe), was intercepted by Borgia's agents.

On March 25, 1498, in the Basilica of Santa Croce, a short distance from here, at the end of Borgo dei Greci, Franciscan friar Francesco di Puglia, during a sermon, challenged anyone who considered Savonarola's excommunication unlawful to undergo a "trial by fire." The essence of this trial was that the participants would walk into a fire, and if God favored one of them, it was presumed He would save the righteous one. Apparently, Brother Francesco did not expect anyone to take up the challenge, as when the Dominican friar

Domenico da Pescia volunteered for the trial by fire, Puglia declared that he would enter the fire only with Savonarola. The latter accepted the challenge, and on the appointed day, he arrived at the Piazza della Signoria, where the fire was being prepared. However, as Savonarola and Pescia awaited Francesco di Puglia, who was hiding in the Palazzo Vecchio, it began to rain, making it impossible to light the fire. Thus, the "victory" in the dispute was awarded to Savonarola.

Nevertheless, supporters of the exiled Medici and the pope had already sentenced the preacher to death. The day after the failed "trial by fire," Girolamo Savonarola was captured by an enraged mob that besieged his San Marco monastery. He was taken to the Palazzo Vecchio for interrogation. Savonarola and two of his fellow Dominican friars were subjected to brutal interrogations and torture carried out by a commission of 17 men appointed by the pope. Ultimately, Savonarola confessed that all his prophecies regarding the pope and the Church were false, and he was condemned to death for heresy. He spent his final days in a cell above the Signoria meeting room in the Palazzo Vecchio, directly under the building's bell tower. On May 23, 1498, Savonarola, along with Dominicans Domenico Buonvicini and Silvestro Maruffi, were hanged in this square before a large crowd. Their bodies were subsequently burned. This act cemented the Medici's return to power in Florence. Today, a round memorial plaque marks the spot where Savonarola and his companions' bodies were burned. You can find it in front of the Neptune Fountain.

Of course, the most famous building in Piazza della Signoria, and indeed in all of Florence, is the Palazzo Vecchio—the "Old Palace." While it is called "Old" now, it was once quite "New," and during the rule of Cosimo I de' Medici, it was known as the "Ducal Palace." After the Tuscan ruler moved his residence across the Arno River to the Pitti Palace in 1565, this architectural masterpiece acquired its current name.

Palazzo Vecchio

Construction of the palace began in 1299, following the suppression of another revolt by an influential family, the Uberti, who sought to seize power in the city. The Florentine craft guilds (or guilds) decreed the confiscation of all the family's property, including the Palazzo dei Fanti and the Palazzo dell'Esecutore di Giustizia (Palace of the Executor of Justice), two palaces located on the site of the current Palazzo Vecchio. To ensure the safety of the Republic's government in the event of another coup attempt, the guilds commissioned the architect Arnolfo di Cambio to design a new palace for the Signoria's meetings. Di Cambio was already renowned for his work on the Basilica of Santa Croce and the Cathedral of Santa Maria del Fiore (the lower part of the facade of which he adorned with sculptures that have not survived to the present day). In his design for the new palace, di Cambio incorporated the old tower of the Foraboschi family; this was slightly extended and integrated into the building's ensemble in 1310 as a bell tower and later (from 1353) as a clock tower. That is why the tower has a slightly offset position; it predates the Palazzo itself.

Gualtieri VI di Brienne. Portrait by Luigi Rubio, 1834.

The tower has held some notable prisoners over the years, including the famous banker Cosimo de' Medici the Elder (who laid the foundations of his family's influence and power in the city but was imprisoned for a time for attempting to conquer the neighboring Republic of Lucca) and the fervent Girolamo Savonarola, whom we have already encountered.

Incidentally, during the time of Savonarola, a radical republican, the palace gained one of Florence's main attractions, the Salone dei Cinquecento ("Hall of the Five Hundred").

This architectural masterpiece in the Mannerist style (in my opinion, somewhat overly ornate), measuring 52 meters (170.7 feet) in length, 23 meters (75 feet) in width, and 18 meters (59 feet) in height, was intended for meetings of the Great Council of the Republic, which comprised 500 members (hence, the hall's name). Besides its size, the hall is notable for having been worked on by Leonardo da Vinci and Michelangelo. It is the only project on which these two great masters collaborated simultaneously. Truth be told, nothing of their frescoes in the "Hall of the Five Hundred" remains: Pope Julius II summoned Michelangelo to work on the famous Sistine Chapel after the latter had made only a few sketches for the hall's frescoes, while da Vinci, though he began the painting, could not complete it. His fresco, "The Battle of Anghiari," depicting the Florentine army battling the Duke of Milan's forces on June 29, 1440, was to be Leonardo's most

monumental work (6.6 x 17.4 m (21.7 x 57 ft)). However, due to da Vinci's unsuccessful experiments with primers and paint mixtures, the fresco began to deteriorate even before its completion. This caused delays that led the Republic's Council to demand either the immediate completion of the painting or the return of the money paid. At the same time, da Vinci was invited to work in Milan, then under French rule, and left his fresco in the "Hall of the Five Hundred" unfinished. Only between 1555 and 1572, during the renovation

Gualtieri VI di Brienne.
Portrait by Luigi Rubio, 1834.

of the hall commissioned by Duke Cosimo I de' Medici and carried out by Giorgio Vasari (whose frescoes adorn the hall today), was Leonardo's work presumably covered or removed. Nonetheless, some hypotheses suggest that Vasari did not destroy the work of the already renowned genius but, instead, concealed it under his "Battle of Marciano," located on the east wall of the hall. You will find it to your right if you face the podium.

Let's return to the broader history of the building. Palazzo Vecchio began serving as the residence of the Signoria and the seat of the Gonfaloniere of Justice as early as 1302, although its exterior and

34

interior appearance evolved over time. For example, in 1342-1343, the Palazzo was expanded toward Via del Ninna, making it resemble a fortress. This period marks the brief rule of Gualtieri VI di Brienne, better known as the Duke of Athens—a title inherited from his crusader ancestors who once conquered the ancient homeland of democracy and established a feudal duchy there.

The fortification and expansion of the Florentine ruler's residence began under di Brienne, who was unpopular among the populace. He openly disregarded the interests of the merchant class and earned a reputation as a notorious despot. Though his harsh tax policies helped Florence recover from a severe crisis, just ten months into his rule, the threat of physical harm loomed over di Brienne, prompting him to leave the city.

The most significant milestones in the history of Palazzo Vecchio are inextricably linked to the Medici family. The "prudent tyrant" Cosimo de' Medici the Elder, who came to lead the Florentine Republic thanks to his immense wealth and the influence it brought, was, despite his ruthless elimination of political opponents and nepotism (awarding state positions to family members), a great patriot and patron of the arts, literature, and architecture. During his time, the Palazzo Vecchio saw the creation of the First Courtyard—one of the building's three courtyards, which you enter through the main gates on Piazza della Signoria. The initial design of the courtyard was by Michelozzo di Bartolomeo Michelozzi (whom Cosimo the Elder also commissioned to decorate the "Hall of Two Hundred," another meeting hall in Palazzo Vecchio). However, most of the courtyard's current decorations were added under Duke Cosimo I, the great-great-grandnephew of Cosimo de' Medici the Elder. For instance, on the occasion of the marriage of Cosimo I's son, Francesco de' Medici, to Archduchess Joanna of Austria (daughter of Emperor Ferdinand I of Habsburg), Vasari was tasked with adorning the courtyard walls with views of Austrian cities (Graz, Innsbruck, Linz, Vienna, Bratislava (Pozsony), Prague, Hall in Tirol, Freiburg im Breisgau, and Konstanz).

Portrait of Cosimo de' Medici.
Workshop of Bronzino. 1565-1569.

But it wasn't just elegant stuccoes, monumental colonnades, marble sculptures, and striking frescoes that adorned Palazzo Vecchio under the Medici. In 1478, a different, more dreadful "decoration" appeared on the windows of this palace. This addition, paradoxically, was quite in keeping with the spirit of the time—a time of flourishing arts, sciences, and humanism. In April 1478, thick ropes hung from the windows of Palazzo Vecchio—once a symbol of the Republic and Florentine democracy — bearing the bodies of Francesco and Jacopo de' Pazzi and Archbishop Francesco Salviati of Pisa. On December 20, 1479, the body of merchant Bernardo di Baroncelli joined them. All these individuals were implicated in a conspiracy against the Medici family, particularly Lorenzo "the Magnificent," who had inherited power in the Republic following the death of his father, Piero "the Unfortunate" (son of Cosimo the Elder). Naturally, the hereditary ruler of the Republic could not avoid being considered a tyrant, and Lorenzo de' Medici was undoubtedly one. However, he also continued the traditions of his grandfather, actively supporting the arts and sciences, and was himself a poet. (It was at Lorenzo's court that the great Botticelli began his rise, for example.) The Pazzi are often described as supporters of democratic freedoms who were destroyed by the Medici, with the participants of that failed conspiracy advocating for their revival. However, as is often the case, the true reasons for the discord between the Pazzi and the Medici were far more mundane. In 1474, Lorenzo de' Medici appointed his son-in-law, Rinaldo Orsini, to the archbishopric of Florence without consulting the Florentines (whose consent was required for the appointment of a new archbishop). Moreover, the Pazzi family had hoped to see their relative, Francesco Salviati, in this position. (Instead, Francesco received the bishopric of Pisa.) Lorenzo de' Medici's less-than-diplomatic actions did not stop there; he had recently fallen out with Pope Sixtus IV, one of the main clients of the Medici Bank, who regularly took loans from it. The cause of their dispute was Imola, a small but strategically located town on the main trade route connecting Florence and Venice. Lorenzo de' Medici had hoped to buy Imola from Duke Galeazzo Maria Sforza of Milan for the colossal sum of 100,000 gold florins. However, at the last moment, Galeazzo Maria sold Imola to the pope for only 40,000. Lorenzo, as the chief banker of the Holy See, refused to facilitate the transaction, prompting Pope Sixtus IV to turn to the Pazzi Bank. Soon, a conspiracy emerged to overthrow the Medici clan. It was led by Francesco de' Pazzi, his uncle Jacopo, their relative Francesco Salviati (Bishop of Pisa), merchant Bernardo Bandini, the likely illegitimate son of Pope Sixtus IV, Girolamo Riario (who became the ruler of Imola), and several others. The pope, although he wrote to the Pazzi that he "could not sanction murder," emphasized that "the Holy See was interested in removing the Medici dynasty from power in Florence" and would "generously reward those who facilitated this." Furthermore, in 2004, it was revealed that Federico da Montefeltro, Duke of Urbino, was also involved in the conspiracy against the Medici. In an encoded letter addressed to the Pazzi and found in the Ubaldini family archives, the duke declared his readiness to station 600 of his soldiers outside Florence and occupy the city at the right moment to prevent a counter-coup by the Medici.

The Pazzi planned to eliminate the city's ruler, Lorenzo, and his brother Giuliano, then occupy Palazzo Vecchio and declare the restoration of the Republic, convene a provisional government, and expel all Medici supporters from the city. Thus, on April 26, 1478, during the Great Mass at Santa Maria del Fiore for Easter, the Pazzi's men attacked the Florentine ruler Lorenzo de' Medici and his brother Giuliano. Francesco Pazzi himself attacked Giuliano with a dagger, inflicting 19 wounds in a frenzy and, in the heat of the attack, accidentally wounding himself. Lorenzo managed to fend off his attackers and take refuge in the cathedral's sacristy. Meanwhile, Francesco

Lorenzo the Magnificent with Florence in the background. Portrait by Girolamo Macchietti, 16th century.

Salviati and his men were supposed to capture Palazzo Vecchio (then called Palazzo della Signoria). However, they were thwarted by Cesare Petrucci, a longtime Medici supporter who had recently been appointed Gonfaloniere of Justice (effectively appointed by Lorenzo). Additionally, to the Pazzi's surprise, the Florentines themselves did not support the uprising; instead, they fiercely defended the Medici family and administered justice against the Pazzi supporters. As a result, Francesco Salviati was captured along with Francesco de' Pazzi on the same day. Both conspirators were sentenced to hanging and, to the cheers of the public, were executed from the windows of Palazzo Vecchio on Piazza della Signoria on April 26, 1478. Later that day, Jacopo de' Pazzi was caught and hanged alongside them; he had tried to escape the city but was overtaken by Medici supporters and, after torture and attempted lynching by the Florentines, was executed. The merchant Bernardo de' Bandini dei Baroncelli, who, along with Francesco Pazzi, had murdered Giuliano de' Medici, also fled. Unlike Jacopo, he managed to make it to Constantinople, where he hoped to seek refuge with the Ottoman Sultan. However, the Sultan ordered Bandini's arrest and return to Florence. Thus, he, too, was hanged from a window of Palazzo Vecchio, dressed in Turkish clothes and sultan's chains. This was how 26-year-old Leonardo da Vinci saw him on Piazza della Signoria. He made a small sketch in his diary—the only remnant of this Florentine merchant.

Following the failure of the Pazzi conspiracy, about 80 people were executed on suspicion of involvement. The Medici made no effort to prevent the Florentines from lynching members and relatives of the Pazzi right in the streets. Once the turmoil had subsided, Lorenzo issued a decree confiscating all property and assets of the Pazzi family, forbidding family members and close relatives from holding public offices, and even banning their use of the Pazzi name. The family was subjected to the ancient Roman practice of *Damnatio Memoriae*—"Damnation of Memory"—whereby the name of the Pazzi was erased from all documents and records, their coats of arms were chiseled off buildings, and so forth. Only after Lorenzo de' Medici's death in 1494 were those family members not directly involved in the conspiracy allowed to return to Florence and reclaim their confiscated property, though they never regained their influence and wealth.

Sometimes, as I stroll through the winding streets of Florence, passing by the Pazzi Palace at Via del Proconsolo 10, I wonder: What if Cosimo de' Medici the Elder had been executed in 1433 after the failed attempt to conquer Lucca? At that time, almost all of Florentine society was opposed to the Medici family. And what if, on Easter Sunday 1478, in the cathedral of Santa Maria del Fiore, Francesco de' Pazzi had attacked Lorenzo first rather than Giuliano? Quite possibly, the tyranny of the Medici could have ended. However, who could guarantee that another ambitious banking family wouldn't have taken their place? And would Florence be the Florence we know today if the blood of the Medici family's enemies did not flow beneath the surface of the city's extraordinary frescoes?

But let us return to Palazzo Vecchio. Before you enter, pay attention to the alternating colored coats of arms beneath the cornice arches. All of them were added to the facade around the same time that Michelozzo di Bartolomeo Michelozzi was working on the decoration of the palace, having been commissioned by Cosimo de' Medici the Elder in the 15th century. Of course, all these coats of arms are directly related to Florence. The first shield on the left depicts a red cross on a white field. This is the so-called "La Croce del Popolo"—"The Cross of the People"—symbolizing civic freedom and popular governance. Next is a red fleur-de-lis on a silver field, the emblem of the Florentine Guelphs (supporters of the pope during the Investiture Controversy), which was established as the official emblem of the Florentine Republic after the expulsion of the Guelphs' opponents, the Ghibellines (whose emblem, a white fleur-de-lis on a crimson field, is located a little farther on). Following this is a divided shield, white and red, symbolizing the union of the cities of Fiesole and Florence. The town of Fiesole, now a municipality within the Florence metropolitan area, was founded more than 300 years before Florence, and its proximity to Dante's city was always perceived by the Florentines as that of a mother and

The hanged Bernardo dei Baroncelli. Sketch by Leonardo da Vinci.

daughter. Next is a shield with two golden keys on a red background, representing the Papal States and indicating Florence's submission to the pope. Immediately following is a blue shield with the golden inscription "Libertas"—"Freedom." It symbolizes Florence's complete independence from anyone. The next coat of arms, preceding the Ghibelline emblem, features a red eagle holding a green dragon in its claws. This represents the Guelph party, which, in any case, ultimately triumphed over the Florentine Ghibellines. It is not hard to guess which side of the conflict each animal symbolizes on this emblem. The last two coats of arms are related to the patrons and protectors of Florence—the French House of Anjou. The first is the coat of arms of Duke Charles of Calabria (1298–1328) and King Robert of Naples (1278–1343), and the second is the coat of arms of King Louis I of Hungary (1342–1382).

Slowly lowering our gaze from the cornice of the Palazzo to the main entrance, we encounter a striking frons, an elegant marble composition adorned with heraldic lilies and lions. The inscriptions decorating it, though executed in 1528 and restored in 1851, hark back to the philosophy of Girolamo Savonarola, who, in 1494, proclaimed Jesus Christ as the "King and Lord of Florence." In the central part, we see the monogram of the Savior: "IHS" ("Jesus Hominum Salvator"—"Jesus, Savior of Men"). Below it, we see His "title": "Rex Regum et Dominus Dominantium" ("King of Kings and Lord of Lords"). Symbolically, for over 300 years, these inscriptions were concealed from public view beneath a panel bearing the coat of arms of the Grand Dukes of Tuscany: the Medici and the Habsburgs.

Sculptures in Piazza della Signoria

After this frons, our attention is captured by the "guardians" of the Palazzo Vecchio. These are two of the most prominent sculptures on Piazza della Signoria, and they have been in dialogue with each other for nearly half a millennium. They converse in a language understood by only a few of the thousands who pass through Piazza della Signoria every day. The first sculpture—Michelangelo's world-renowned "David"—is, of course, a copy. It is an extraordinarily precise and excellent replica of the original, which is deservedly housed in its own room at the Accademia Gallery. This copy was installed here in 1910, nearly 40 years after the original "David" was moved under the museum dome to protect it from the elements. But let us momentarily set aside formalities, especially because this copy is almost indistinguishable from Michelangelo's masterpiece.

What do you see when you look at this sculpture? On a literal level, you see the Old Testament hero, the future King of Judah, the conqueror of the giant Goliath. Here he is, the handsome youth who chose not to don armor before facing the Philistines, holding a leather sling over his shoulder and gripping the fateful stone in his right hand.

But doesn't it seem that something is off about this hand? While David's entire body displays calm and confidence, his hand, with its bulging veins, is large, rough, even somewhat disproportionate, and tense. If you stare at this hand for a while, it might even seem that it does not belong to David. Perhaps this impression will not be misleading.

If you have ever visited the Sistine Chapel in the Vatican and seen Michelangelo's incredible frescoes on its ceiling and walls, you likely remember two figures among the many depicted there: the figure of Jesus executing the Last Judgment and the figure of Adam receiving life from the Lord. Michelangelo began work on these frescoes almost immediately after completing his "David" and leaving Florence again. (The great creator had also worked in Rome before "David," on the famous "Vatican Pietà.")

What if I told you that Michelangelo connected these three figures—David, Adam, and Jesus—into a single message? This might sound a bit strange, but look closely at their hands. The raised, tense, veined hand of Jesus, who is executing the Last Judgment, is raised in a gesture typically used by ancient orators (e.g., Raphael's "School of Athens") to indicate dialogue. In addition, in Byzantine iconographic tradition, this gesture symbolizes blessing (which we see in many Byzantine icons of Christ). Adam's gesture, reaching out to the Lord who grants him life, can be interpreted as accepting a blessing, while David's lowered hand can be seen as a gesture of humility. Thus, each of these three hands points to the figure of the Lord, emphasizing His unseen (or quite visible, in the case of the Sistine Chapel frescoes) presence in each of the stories that Michelangelo depicts. David, defeating Goliath by slinging a stone with his right hand, enabled the advance of the Israelite armies against the Philistines and predetermined the expulsion of the latter from the land of Israel.

The sculpture also has an underlying context: The Republic commissioned this colossal figure in 1501 during the revival of Florentine democracy when the Medici family was in exile and all power was once again in the hands of elected officials. In this sense, the youthful David, casting his determined gaze at the titan Goliath, symbolizes the long-awaited revival of civic freedoms, the laying of the foundation for a new state, the liberation of Florence from long-standing tyranny, and a new dawn of democracy. He embodies the young society of Florence, unafraid to challenge the "monster" that the Medici clan represented.

It is all the more intriguing that Michelangelo's "David" was meant to be balanced by a sculpture of Hercules slaying the fire-breathing giant Cacus, the son of the ancient Roman god Vulcan—unlike "David," a completely opaque allusion to the political events of early 16th-century Florence. Indeed, this is the composition we see today: David faces it with a fearless and slightly contemptuous gaze. However, Michelangelo did not create this sculpture; he received the commission for it in 1508, but a suitable block of marble could not be found, causing Buonarroti to turn to other projects. In the meantime, the Medici family regained control of Florence in 1512, thus ending the period of "Second Democracy." In 1523, the new ruler of the city, Cardinal Giulio de' Medici (who became Pope Clement VII that same year and transferred power to his brother, Ippolito de' Medici), commissioned the sculpture from Baccio Bandinelli (1493-1560). It took Bandinelli nine years to complete the work (from 1527 to 1530; the Medici were again expelled from Florence, along with Bandinelli, causing the project to be halted). Upon completion, the sculpture, under the unchallenged rule of the Medici, came to symbolize the opposite phenomenon: Hercules was seen here as the embodiment of brute force and power overcoming the "chaos of lawlessness" represented by the monstrous offspring of Vulcan. (According to legend, Cacus stole four cows and four bulls from Hercules while he slept—another intriguing metaphor.) Almost immediately after its completion, the sculpture provoked a storm of criticism: it was deemed ugly, crude, and vague in both composition and plasticity. Indeed, much of the criticism directed at the sculpture was, in fact, criticism of the Medici family. (The first Florentine duke Alessandro de' Medici even imprisoned those who made particularly scathing comments about the sculpture). However, it cannot be denied that Bandinelli, trying to emulate Michelangelo, was deeply enraged by his competitor's talent. Thus, unlike Michelangelo, who signed his work only once, Bandinelli placed a deliberately prominent inscription on the pedestal of "Hercules and Cacus" to indicate his authorship.

As for the other sculptures in the square, they are far from random. For example, to the left of "David" stands a bronze statue of Judith beheading Holofernes—another Old Testament scene telling the story of the pious Jewish widow who saved her city from Assyrian invaders by decapitating their proud and debauched general, Holofernes, who had desired to share a bed with her. The symbolism of this sculpture, created by Donatello on the commission of Cosimo de' Medici the Elder, is apparent: Florence, standing against numerous external enemies (Milan, France, and others), is depicted as the pious Judith, who, through faith and love for her homeland, overcomes all enemies. Originally, this sculpture was housed in the Palazzo Vecchio, but during Savonarola's rule, it was moved to the square for public display. After that, the composition began to be interpreted as a symbol of "victory over the tyranny of the Medici." In subsequent years, the sculpture was moved around the square: to the inner courtyard of the Palazzo Vecchio and to the Loggia dei Lanzi. In 1919, it was installed on the left side of the palace. In 1988, the original Donatello work was returned to the Palazzo Vecchio, and a precise copy was situated in its place on the square.

We must not forget the copy of Donatello's "Marzocco". This famous symbol of Florence—the vigilant guardian of the city who holds a shield with the Florentine lily in its paw and whose nickname literally means "Little Mars"—is a noteworthy figure. The original sculpture, which is now displayed in the Donatello Hall of the Bargello Museum, was commissioned by the Republic's government in 1420. It was intended to adorn the apartments of Pope Martin V, who, during his visit to Florence, stayed at the Monastery of Santa Maria Novella. In 1812, the sculpture was moved to Piazza della Signoria, but by 1885, it had been replaced by a copy, and Donatello's work was transferred to the museum.

As a symbol of Florence, the "Marzocco" has a lengthy history, and its connection to the god of war, Mars, is not incidental. According to ancient Roman astrology, Mars governs the zodiac sign of Leo, and the first stone lion guardian could have appeared in the city as early as the 14th century at the entrance to the Ponte Vecchio. In 1333, after a flood destroyed the ancient statue of Mars that had stood there since time immemorial, the townspeople decided to replace it with "Little Mars."

Another significant sculptural composition in the square is the "Fountain of Neptune," which we previously mentioned during our discussion of Girolamo Savonarola. (The spot where Savonarola was executed is located next to the fountain.) This fountain was commissioned by the Grand Duke Cosimo I de' Medici, whom we already know, and it, along with the First Courtyard of the Palazzo Vecchio, was ordered to commemorate the marriage of his son, Ferdinand, to the Austrian Archduchess Joanna in 1559. The project was designed by the same Baccio Bandinelli, but it was executed by his student, Bartolomeo Ammannati, who also emulated Michelangelo's style and is perhaps best known for the Jesuit College building in Rome.

The addition of the equestrian statue of Cosimo I de' Medici by Jean de Boullogne (or, as he is colloquially known in Florence, Giambologna) in 1594 led to an unexpected context: The two sculptures could now be interpreted as symbols of the expansionist ambitions of the first Grand Duke of Tuscany (Cosimo I) on land and at sea. The statue was commissioned by Ferdinand I, the "grateful son" of Cosimo. The pedestal of the statue features bas-reliefs depicting scenes from the life of the deceased ruler: his triumphant entry into the defeated Siena and the coronation of Cosimo as the Grand Duke of Tuscany in Rome.

Another work by Giambologna on the Piazza della Signoria—the "Rape of the Sabine Women" (1582) in the Loggia dei Lanzi—has far less meaning than it might initially appear to have. The block of marble that Giambologna chose for this composition was the largest ever brought to Florence, and the sculptor's intention was simply to demonstrate his virtuosity in working with stone, which he undoubtedly achieved: "The Rape of the Sabine Women" became the first sculpture in the history of European art that should be viewed from multiple angles. The subject depicted in marble recounts a scene from the mythological history of Rome. According to legend, in ancient times, the city was inhabited only by men. To remedy this, the founder and King of Rome, Romulus, organized a grand festival, inviting neighboring Latin and Sabine families. In the midst of the

celebration, the Romans seized their guests and abducted all the women. Enraged, the Sabines and Latins waged a brutal and lengthy war, which ceased only when the Sabine women, now accustomed to their Roman husbands, intervened during one of the battles, pleading for peace and persuading both sides to reconcile. According to legend, this led to the formation of a new kingdom where Romans, Latins, and Sabines lived in harmony under Romulus's rule.

Of course, we must not forget the masterpiece by Benvenuto Cellini—"Perseus with the Head of Medusa." This exquisite work of art depicts the ancient Greek hero Perseus, son of Zeus and the Argive princess Danaë, who set out on a mission from King Polydectes to obtain the head of Medusa, the Gorgon whose gaze could turn anyone to stone. It is important to note that Medusa, once a beautiful maiden with long, lovely hair, was violently pursued by the sea god Poseidon. In an attempt to escape Poseidon's advances, Medusa fled to the temple of Athena, where Poseidon found and assaulted her. And, of course, it was not Poseidon—the brother of Zeus and Hades—who was punished for this monstrous crime. Rather, it was the unfortunate Medusa whom the gods blamed for "desecrating the temple of Athena." As a result, Athena herself disfigured Medusa, turning her once-beautiful face into a hideous visage and her lovely hair into serpents. Ultimately, Athena, along with Hermes and Hephaestus, helped Perseus behead the tormented Medusa; they provided him with a shield that allowed him to view Medusa's reflection and thereby avoid her direct gaze while approaching her.

Now that you are aware of the backstory behind Cellini's depicted scene, consider the context of its creation. It was the year 1530; after yet another three-year exile, during which democracy had been briefly restored in Florence, the Medici, with the support of Emperor Charles V, returned to the city. Pope Clement VII (Julius Medici) transformed Florence into a duchy and elevated his illegitimate son, Alessandro, to the throne. Thus, any attempts to restore popular sovereignty in the city came to an end, and soon, almost all of Tuscany was under the control of the all-powerful banking family. In 1545, Alessandro's distant relative and heir, Cosimo I, commissioned Benvenuto Cellini to create this sculpture, intended to affirm the triumph of the valiant and beautiful demigod Perseus—symbolizing order and divine will (as Athena herself guided his hand in the battle with Medusa, akin to Michelangelo's "David")—over the chaos and madness of the republic's past embodied by the Gorgon. The idea for this composition came from Cosimo I himself, as Cellini noted in his memoirs. Art became a means by which the Medici legitimized their tyranny, a tool to promote the notion that freedom was dangerous and unnecessary. They enforced this celestial beauty, created by artists under their patronage, with iron and blood throughout Tuscany.

In addition to these sculptures, the Loggia dei Lanzi houses remarkable, though lesser-known, and somewhat later works by Giambologna, such as "Hercules and the Centaur" (1599) and "The Rape of Polyxena" by Pio Fedi (1865). There are also several ancient statues of women, among which we identify only Agrippina the Younger (sister of Caligula), Marciana (sister of Trajan), Matidia (mother-in-law of Hadrian), and Tusnelda (wife of the Cheruscan leader Arminius, who achieved a famous victory over the Romans in the Battle of the Teutoburg Forest in AD 9). Another relatively ancient piece is "Menelaus with the Body of Patroclus," which depicts heroes from Homeric epics. It was made in the 1st century AD from an earlier original and restored in the 16th century under the commission of Cosimo I, who purchased it in Rome. Also dating to the 1st century AD is the right of the two "Medici Lions" at the entrance to the Loggia dei Lanzi. Commissioned by Grand Duke Ferdinand I of Tuscany, the second lion was made in imitation of the ancient one by the sculptor Flaminio Vacca in 1600. The lion holding a sphere symbolizes a vigilant, tireless guardian; should it loosen its grip even slightly, the sphere will roll away and shatter. Moreover, these lions resonate well with the earlier (or, rather, later) depiction of the "Marzocco" by Donatello.

Orsanmichele Church and Museum

It is time to leave Piazza della Signoria, no matter how difficult it might be to part with the masterpieces of sculpture in the Loggia dei Lanzi or to leave the Hall of the Five Hundred in Palazzo Vecchio. Awaiting us is via dei Calzaiuoli, which has a delightful surprise in store: After crossing two intersections (with Via della Condotta and Via dei Lamberti/Via dei Cimatori), we will find ourselves between two churches, one of which will undoubtedly surpass the other. To your left will be Orsanmichele, towering majestically, and to your right will be the relatively modest San Carlo dei Lombardi. The latter is a typical example of 14th-century Florentine Gothic, despised by both Giotto and Brunelleschi. It was erected in memory of the expulsion of the Duke of Athens from the city (as we discussed in detail earlier). Notably, one of the architects who worked on this church, Benci di Cione Dami (a member of the renowned Florentine

54

family that produced four notable masters), oversaw the construction of the Loggia dei Lanzi in 1382 and the reconstruction of Orsanmichele in 1361 and 1369. This church, which was alternately dedicated to Saint Anne and Saint Michael, was originally built in 1349. After being handed over to the Compagnia di San Carlo dei Lombardi (a national guild of Lombard merchants and craftsmen residing in Florence), the church was renamed in honor of Saint Charles Borromeo (1538–1584), the leader of the Catholic Counter-Reformation.

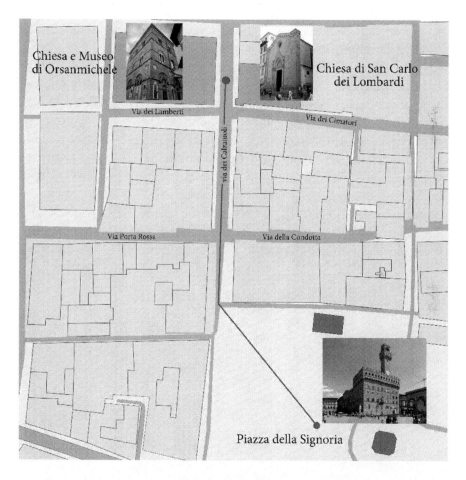

On the site of Orsanmichele once stood a convent with extensive gardens and orchards. The name of the church reflects its origins. "Or. San Michele"—the "Oratory of Saint Michael"—can also be read as

"San Michele in Orto," meaning "Saint Michael in the Garden." This name originally belonged to a small 8th-century church on the site of which began construction of a large grain market—known as the "Loggia del Grano" (from the Italian word "grano," meaning grain)— in 1240. This market succeeded the old city bazaar, from which the name of this part of Florence, Mercato Vecchio, derives, occupying the area of the ancient Roman forum. Indeed, the Loggia del Grano is what you see before you. Yes, this building was not originally intended as a church: The lower open colonnade housed bakeries, while the upper floors (to protect against theft and moisture) served as granaries. The special "grain chutes"—channels within the columns through which grain was poured down from the granaries— are still beautifully preserved in the interior of the current Orsanmichele church. On one of the pilasters of the arcade's lower floor, there once stood a revered miraculous image of the Virgin Mary, probably transferred from an older monastery or church. To manage Florentines' donations in honor of this image, the Compagnia dei Laudesi, or the Company of Orsanmichele, was established. Franciscan and Dominican monks frequently criticized this company for "collaborating with idolatry." The company's headquarters, at the corner of via de' Calzaiuoli 21 and via dei Lamberti 1, still stands, and you can still see various emblems of the organization on its facades. Although the company began to decline in the mid-14th century, it existed until 1752.

As for Orsanmichele itself, its transformation into a church was, in a way, prompted by a fire on July 10, 1304. This fire caused severe damage to the "Grain Loggia." Following the disaster, a decision was made to reconstruct it such that each of the city's guilds would "take responsibility for a column of the Loggia and create a figure of their patron saint within it, and on the saints' feast days, the craftsmen would make donations in their honor, from which the Compagnia di San Michele d'Orto would distribute aid to the poor." In reality, work did not commence until 30 years later, and the project continued until 1406, when the crown-like pinnacle of the building was completed. Like San Carlo dei Lombardi, the history of Orsanmichele is linked to the expulsion of the despotic ruler Gualtieri VI di Brienne, Duke of Athens, from Florence. Because the trade and craft guilds were long considered the main "pillars" of democracy in the Republic, their actions led to the tyrant's overthrow and banishment from the city in 1343. On July 26 of the same year, the feast day of Saint Anne, the decision was made to adorn Orsanmichele with banners bearing the guilds' coats of arms and to display them annually on this day in honor of Florence's merchants and craftsmen.

All the statues you see today on the facades of Orsanmichele are replicas of the original works by the great masters of their time (Donatello, Ghiberti, Nanni di Banco, and others). There are 14 statues in total, each depicting the patron saint of one of the 14 Florentine guilds (butchers, armorers, shoemakers, etc.). Additionally, among the magnificent Gothic vaults of the ground floor, four tondi (medallions made of glazed terracotta or majolica) depicting the guilds' coats of arms have been preserved: those of the silk merchants (two putti holding a shield with gates depicted), the doctors and apothecaries (Madonna with Child), the butchers (putti holding a shield with a goat depicted), and the stone and wood workers (an axe). Inside the church, the luxurious tabernacle (from the Latin "tabernaculum"—booth, tent) is a reminder of the "Black Death" epidemic that struck Florence in 1348. When the plague arrived, desperate Florentines seeking salvation began to make donations to Orsanmichele in penance and to atone for their sins. They hoped to escape divine retribution, which they believed was the cause of the horrific epidemic. Ultimately, the parish accumulated 350,000 florins—the annual budget of the Republic—and this entire sum was used in 1349 to commission the tabernacle from the renowned master Andrea Orcagna, who spent ten years on this stunning work.

Piazza della Repubblica

If you turn off via dei Calzaiuoli onto via degli Speziali, you will soon arrive at Piazza della Repubblica—third in importance, after Piazza del Duomo and Piazza della Signoria, among the squares of Florence. Long ago, it was known as the Market Square because it housed the city's main marketplace, extending up to the area of Orsanmichele. This market, in turn, was established on the site of the ancient Roman forum—a classical center of any city in Ancient Rome. The forum housed the principal administrative and religious buildings and was intersected by two major roads in any Roman fortified settlement: the cardo (running from north to south) and the decumanus (crossing the cardo from west to east). Today, the locations of the cardo are represented by via Roma, via Calimala, and via Por Santa Maria, running sequentially from the Arno riverbank to Piazza del Duomo. The decumanus is now represented by via del Corso, via degli

Speziali, and via degli Strozzi. Thus, these six streets, which continue one after the other, are among the oldest in the city and have retained their direction for over 2000 years. The intersection of these two main streets of Roman Florence is still marked by the "Column of Abundance"—the only medieval monument, albeit restored, on this square.

By the Middle Ages, the once-spacious forum square had become so densely built up that, according to chroniclers, "there was no space left for gardens or pasture." Due to the lack of space, residential buildings had to be extended with additional floors. Despite this, the square, now known as the Market Square, remained the main meeting place for Florentines and one of the three central locations in the city, alongside the spiritual center (Piazza del Duomo) and the administrative center (Piazza della Signoria).

From the 13th century onward, the part of the city adjacent to the market, now situated between via dei Brunelleschi, via dei Pecori, and via Roma, began to decline rapidly. After the Guelphs were expelled from Florence, this district suffered heavily from fires and was looted. Thus, it was considered a "disreputable" area. By the 15th century, although noble Florentine families owned the land and many buildings, most of the houses were occupied by brothels, taverns, and people of "less respectable habits." This determined the fate of the district in the 16th century, when Sephardic Jews fleeing the Inquisition from Spain began arriving in Tuscany. Grand Duke Cosimo I de' Medici and his son Francesco ordered all these Jews to be settled in this very district. Local Italian Jews were also relocated there, thus forming the Florentine Jewish ghetto. The district was enclosed by a wall and, thanks to the Jewish community, which took care of order, cleanliness, and the welfare of its "city within a city", it underwent a transformation.

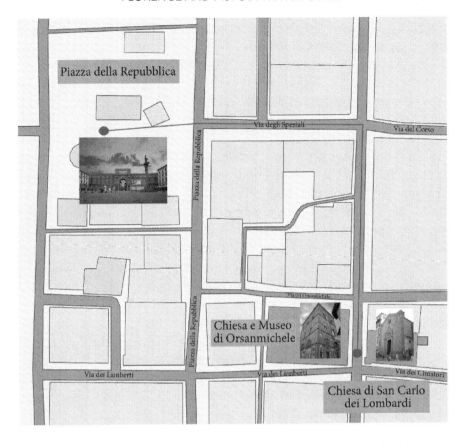

On the square itself (which became known as the Old Market Square in the 16th century due to the construction of the new Market Loggia near Ponte Vecchio), many ancient churches were preserved for a long time. However, these were demolished in the 19th century during a reorganization of the area.

After the 1848 revolution, Florentine Jews were emancipated, and most of them left the ghetto. Subsequently, dubious characters once again overran the district. The horrendous sanitary conditions and poor reputation of the places therein led the city municipality to order the demolition of the old quarters of Piazza di Mercato Vecchio (the Old Market Square); that demolition began in the 1880s. Of course, along with the slums and dreadful tenements that harbored prostitution and criminal activities, significant historical landmarks were demolished: churches, ancient mansions of noble families, and medieval towers. Among the great works of art that once stood in the market square, only Giorgio Vasari's Loggia del Pesce was preserved. It was carefully dismantled and moved to Piazza dei Ciompi. Later, after a statue of the first King of united Italy, Vittorio Emanuele II, was erected there, the square was renamed in his honor but was often simply called "Piazza Vittorio." After the 1946 referendum, which abolished the monarchy, the square was renamed to honor the Republic, though Florentines called it by its old name for some time. By the way, the statue of King Vittorio Emanuele II was also relocated and now stands at the entrance to Cascine Park.

Piazza della Repubblica features primarily 19th-century architectural monuments. One of them is the "Trianon" palace, which combines various elements of Renaissance architecture and serves as a sort of "quintessence of Italian revival." This palace houses the famous department store "La Rinascente." Between the "Trianon" and the rather unremarkable and controversial building of the headquarters of the "Banca di Sicilia" is the barely noticeable "Torre Romaldelli"—a reconstructed copy of a 13th-century building that once stood on this very spot and belonged to the renowned Romaldelli family. The arch of this tower leads to a small inner square—Piazza dei Tre Re or "Square of the Three Kings," named after an ancient inn that had existed here since the 14th century. In those times, this "square" was more of a private courtyard and the heart of the Macci family's estate, whose seven-century-old, four-story mansion greets you when you enter Piazza dei Tre Re.

Another notable building on the square is the palazzo delle Giubbe Rosse or "Palace of the Red Coats," which appears to be composed of three distinct parts.

The palace received its name from the café " Le Giubbe Rosse" (" The Red Coats"), which opened here in 1897 as a Bavarian brewery under the name " Reininghaus." The brewery quickly became very popular among Florentines. Because the waiters wore red jackets in the Viennese fashion, and the German name was complex, locals preferred to say, " andiamo da quelli delle giubbe rosse" —" let's go to those in red coats." When a café and a chess club replaced the brewery, the old nickname became the official name of the establishment. In the ensuing years, it received visits from many notable personalities, including André Gide, Gordon Craig, and Vladimir Lenin. If you walk around the back of the palace, you will find that it "absorbs" an older building: the palazzo dei Catellini da Castiglione (whose corner is visible from via dei Cavalieri). This palace, built perhaps in the 13th to 14th centuries, belonged to a prominent Florentine family and was partially demolished and partially restored to be incorporated into the new building. This happened at the end of the 19th century during the reorganization of the Old Market Square.

The undisputed dominant feature of the square and its main "background" is the majestic palazzo dell'Arcone di Piazza, whose two wings are connected by a large arch. This palace was also built on the site of medieval buildings, which are now remembered only through old photographs, daguerreotypes, and drawings. As a symbol of the destruction of the medieval Market Square heritage, the palace was long criticized for being "excessively pompous" and possessing a "distinctly non-Florentine, more Roman character". As a result, in the early 1930s, one of the most sought-after Italian architects of the time, Marcello Piacentini, proposed a project to demolish the arch and simplify the facades of the resulting two buildings. For some reason, however, this plan was not realized, and the palace has been restored only twice (in 1980 and 2022).

Giotto's Bell Tower

Now, let's walk a bit farther down Via Roma and turn right at the first intersection onto Via dei Tosinghi, then return to the already familiar Via dei Calzaiuoli, which will lead us straight to Piazza del Duomo. However, before we reach the end, let's pause for a moment at the turn onto Vicolo degli Adimari. Get ready to witness a true marvel. Walk cautiously until the yellowish house on the corner of Via dei Calzaiuoli fades away and Giotto di Bondone's bell tower reveals itself—the herald, faithful companion, and eternal guardian of Santa Maria del Fiore. This bell tower is the junction of geometry, painting, and music, the creation of a brilliant architect who managed to draft a detailed project but completed only the first tier before his death.

As you get closer, you'll see numerous relief medallions—hexagons and diamonds—which, along with the statues on the third tier and the sharp boundary lines between them, form a stunning geometric symphony. Each medallion, of course, has its own story. To read the images in the diamonds, you should start from the West façade (facing Piazza di San Giovanni). There, you can observe: God creating Adam; the creation of Eve; their hard labor after their expulsion from Eden; the invention of animal husbandry by Jabal (a descendant of Adam and Eve); the invention of musical instruments by Jubal (Jabal's brother); and the invention of metallurgy by Tubal-cain (half-brother of Jabal and Jubal). My favorite scene is the drunken Noah lying under a tree after planting grapes and making the first wine following the Great Flood.

Next, we move to the South façade, where we see: Noah's fourth son, Ionitus, who, according to the Old Testament, invented astronomy; the art of construction (an unidentified but substantial master and two apprentices building a stone tower); medicine (a healer diagnosing a patient's urine, contained in a vessel he holds in his hand); hunting; weaving; lawmaking (another link between Florence and Ancient Greece: This medallion depicts the mythical King of Peloponnesus, Phoroneus, who gave people their first laws); and, finally, Daedalus as the " father of mechanics" —the mythical inventor of wings and builder of the legendary Labyrinth on the island of Crete, home to the Minotaur.

On the East façade, you can observe navigation and Hercules with his club (with which he killed Cacus at Palazzo Vecchio). The exact meaning of Hercules is difficult to determine, but it is believed that he symbolizes either civil liberties or justice—quite debatable, in my opinion. Behind him, we see men plowing the land with oxen, representing agriculture. As for the next medallion, I bet you will never guess its meaning: a man riding in a cart pulled by two mares. Carriage drivers? No, not them. Horse breeders? Wrong again. And no, not even couriers. Strangely enough, it represents theatrical art. If you guessed it right the first time, allow me to mentally shake your hand. The mythical founder of the theatrical acting profession—an ancient Greek named Thespis—traveled from town to town in a cart, giving performances directly from it. The last medallion on the East side depicts Euclid with a compass in hand, symbolizing architecture, which is inconceivable without geometric measurements.

On the North side, we find: the ancient Greek sculptor Polykleitos; the ancient Greek painter Apelles; either the Roman grammarian Priscian of Caesarea (author of an 18-volume grammar of the Latin language) or Aelius Donatus (a grammarian and rhetorician known as the teacher of Saint Jerome of Stridon); Plato and Aristotle debating, representing dialectics; Orpheus, symbolizing musical art; Pythagoras and Euclid (again), representing arithmetic and geometry, which go hand in hand; and, finally, what is believed to be Ptolemy, symbolizing either astrology or astronomy but inexplicably depicted with a hammer and anvil.

Of course, these medallions are not original. The originals are housed in the Museo dell'Opera del Duomo (Museum of the Works of the Cathedral), and these precise replicas were installed in their place in the last century. The same applies to the diamonds and the sculptures on the third tier of the campanile.

The seven diamonds on the second tier on the North side depict the seven sacraments of the Church: baptism, confession, marriage, holy orders, confirmation, Eucharist, and anointing of the sick. The four sculptures on this side represent the Tiburtine Sibyl (an ancient prophetess who foretold the birth of Christ), King David, King

Solomon, and the Erythraean Sibyl (another prophetess who taught divination to the Etruscans).

The diamonds on the East side represent the Seven Liberal Arts (those pursued by free people in antiquity, as opposed to mechanical arts, which were the domain of slaves): grammar, dialectic, and rhetoric (trivium) and arithmetic, music, geometry, and astronomy (quadrivium). The sculptures on this side, with the exception of one ("Abraham Sacrifices Isaac"), are rather tentatively identified; they are likely the prophets Malachi, Zechariah, and Isaiah.

Moving to the South side, we see diamonds depicting the theological virtues: faith, hope, and charity. Additionally, we find the cardinal virtues: prudence, justice, temperance, and fortitude. Among the sculptures, which also depict Old Testament prophets, only one can be identified with certainty: the first one, which is Moses.

Finally, let's look at the West side of the campanile. Here, the diamonds represent the seven planets of the Solar System: the Moon (then considered a planet), Mercury, Venus, the Sun (also considered a planet), Mars, Jupiter, and Saturn. The sculptures on this side again depict prophets: Daniel, Habakkuk, Jeremiah, and Obadiah.

The construction of the entire campanile took 25 years. From 1334 to 1337, it was overseen by Giotto himself. After his death, the project was continued by Andrea Pisano, for whom the campanile of the Duomo also became a lifelong endeavor; he died of the plague in 1348, after which the construction of the campanile was halted until 1351, when Francesco Talenti took over. Talenti completed the last three tiers of the bell tower with Gothic windows and a large, projecting terrace instead of a spire.

Today, the campanile houses seven bells, the oldest of which, "Campanone," was cast in 1705.

Santa Maria del Fiore

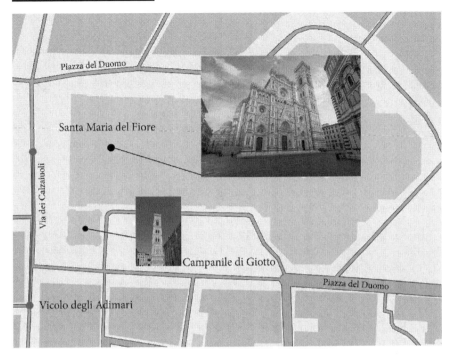

Now, let us stand before the facade of the Cathedral of Florence—the city's main attraction, one of Italy's symbols, and a pinnacle of the Italian Renaissance. This is not just a church, not just a cathedral, not just an architectural masterpiece, but a true manifesto of Florence. For almost 600 years, it has stood tall over the city, dominating it and allowing no other building to surpass it in significance or grandeur. "Beauty will save the world," wrote the great Dostoevsky, and Santa Maria del Fiore seems to declare this with its sheer majesty. How many rulers has Florence seen in its history, how many dukes, gonfaloniers, captains, margraves, and podestas, how many states have been born and disappeared around it, how many republics, duchies, and kingdoms have come and gone, all seemingly flowing away with the waters of the Arno into the distant sea, while the immutable beauty, frozen in stone on this square, remains eternal?

Several generations of craftsmen worked on this cathedral, led by the finest masters of their time. The first stone of Santa Maria del Fiore was laid by Arnolfo di Cambio, who completed a large-scale brick model of the future cathedral in 1296. (Later models of the facades made of wood and stone are now housed in the Museo dell'Opera del Duomo). After he died in 1302, construction halted for 30 years until the wool merchants' guild took over financing and entrusted the project to Giotto di Bondone, who enlisted Andrea Pisano as his assistant. Following Giotto's death in 1337, Pisano continued to work on Santa Maria del Fiore with the help of other masters such as Andrea Orcagna and Neri di Fioravante. However, Pisano fell victim to the plague, which claimed the lives of more than half of Florence's population in 1348. Following the end of the epidemic, Francesco Talenti was appointed chief architect in 1349, but he managed to complete only Giotto's campanile. The cathedral itself was completed (except for the dome) by 1418.

FILIPPO BRVNELLESCHI SCVL. E. ARCHIT.
FIORENTINO

Filippo Brunelleschi

The dome posed significant challenges. A dome of the size required for the colossal cathedral (which remains one of the largest Christian churches in the world) would have collapsed if built according to classical methods. While Gothic architects had effectively addressed roofing for such large structures, the Gothic style was considered barbaric by Renaissance masters who worked predominantly in the Romanesque style (from the word "Rome"). According to an established legend in art history, the eminent architect Filippo Brunelleschi presented his dome design to the Florentine Signoria (government) and, for simplicity, brought a boiled egg with him. "Can you make it stand upright?" he asked the officials. "No," they replied. Brunelleschi then tapped the bottom of the egg on the table and stood it on the resulting dent: "This is how I will set the dome," he concluded. While this story sounds apocryphal, the fact remains that Brunelleschi succeeded in building the dome.

The dome is protected from collapse by a pointed, cone-shaped internal framework onto which the external, visible dome is essentially "fitted." This framework bears the weight of the structure and transfers it to the building's walls, while the inner vault of the dome, 91 meters above the floor, rests on this framework without issue. Brunelleschi was involved in every stage of the dome's preparation and construction. He also invented innovative mechanisms and devices for lifting the dome's components to a significant height. In the workshop of his teacher Andrea del Verrocchio (who later worked on the golden sphere topping the lantern of the dome), the young Leonardo da Vinci had the opportunity to see some of Brunelleschi's inventions and sketch them in his notebooks. This led to the long-held belief that these inventions were Leonardo's rather than Brunelleschi's.

It is worth noting that this is the largest brick dome in the world. Brunelleschi and his craftsmen used approximately four million bricks of various shapes and sizes to line its interior.

A competition was held among all Florentine engineers and architects to design the lantern for the dome. This was similar to the earlier contest for the dome itself. Unsurprisingly, Brunelleschi won again. His design for the lantern was the logical completion of his dome, as it continued the octagonal shape of the main structure. However, Brunelleschi did not live to see his brilliant creation crowned with the lantern; he died just two months after the competition. Another renowned architect, Michelozzo, completed the lantern, while the large gilded copper sphere at the top was crafted in the workshop of Andrea del Verrocchio, the teacher of Leonardo da Vinci, Sandro Botticelli, Domenico Ghirlandaio, Pietro Perugino, and many other famous Renaissance artists. Unfortunately, the original sphere no longer sits atop the dome; it fell twice during storms (in 1492 and

1600) and was replaced by a sturdier, larger one. A marble disc on the rear side of Piazza del Duomo marks the site of the last fall.

The observation balcony, or ballatoio, on the southeast side of the cathedral was added in the early 16th century by Baccio d'Agnolo and Antonio da Sangallo the Elder. The reason this balcony doesn't encircle the entire cathedral is quite comical. During its construction, Michelangelo was in Florence, and when asked his opinion of the work of d'Agnolo and da Sangallo, the great master remarked, "It makes the cathedral dome look like a cricket cage." Consequently, the work was halted. Michelangelo's comment referenced a well-known Florentine tradition, the "Festival of Crickets," held on Ascension Day to mark the arrival of spring. During this festival, people gathered in Cascine Park and gave each other cages with live crickets for good luck. (Today, mechanical crickets are used instead.) The origins of this tradition are unclear, with three hypotheses: crickets awakening in spring heralding summer, a historical method of pest control, and a romantic story of two youths giving crickets to a girl to symbolize their desire to be "imprisoned" with her.

Returning to Santa Maria del Fiore, let us stand before the entrance of this magnificent cathedral and gaze at its facade. The incredible number of intricate, fine details, each carrying its own significance and telling part of a larger story, combine to create a unique symphony in stone. However, this facade is not the one that the architects originally envisioned, nor is it the one that Michelangelo and Leonardo da Vinci saw. The current facade is less than 150 years old. The original facade was incomplete at the cathedral's consecration by Pope Eugene IV on March 25, 1436, and it remained that way for many decades, even centuries. The lower part was adorned with marble and sculptures (a reconstruction of this part of the old facade can be seen in the Museo dell'Opera del Duomo), but most of it was left as bare bricks. Lorenzo the Magnificent held a competition to complete the facade, but nothing was decided. In 1587, under Grand Duke Francesco I de' Medici, the unfinished facade was dismantled entirely. Several projects for a new facade were proposed, the most famous being the Baroque design by Gerardo Silvani in 1636 (on display in the Museo dell'Opera del Duomo). However, none were accepted. Santa Maria del Fiore remained in this unpresentable state until the 19th century. Two more competitions were held. Finally, in 1870, Emilio De Fabris's design was approved, and he was officially appointed the "architect of the Florence Cathedral facade." The project was expensive, and funding came largely from wealthy Florentines, including the Russian aristocrat and millionaire Pavel Pavlovich Demidov, Prince of San Donato. The Demidov coat of arms can be seen on the facade to the right of the main entrance, among the heraldic shields of other donors.

While we won't detail each of the numerous sculptures adorning this beautiful facade, we should note a few important ones. The two main statues flanking the central entrance depict the patron saints of Florence: Saint Reparata and Saint Zenobius. The four large statues on the second tier, corresponding to the nave boundaries, represent church hierarchs directly associated with the cathedral's construction. From left to right, these are Cardinal Pietro Valeriani, who participated in laying the cathedral's foundation stone; Bishop Agostino Tinacci, who blessed the laying of the columns in 1357; Pope Eugene IV, who consecrated the cathedral in 1436; and Archbishop of Florence Saint Antoninus, who blessed the start of the dome's construction and the lantern's completion.

At the top of the facade are busts of distinguished Florentines, each symbolizing a particular science or craft in which they excelled. For instance, Amerigo Vespucci represents geography and history. Yes, the man after whom two continents (North and South America) are named, who proved that Christopher Columbus had discovered a new continent rather than a shortcut to India, was a native of Florence. His relative's wife, Simonetta Vespucci, is believed to be the model for Sandro Botticelli's "The Birth of Venus."

Now, let's step inside. These vaults have witnessed so many incredible historical events that it's hard to choose just one as an example. Here, in front of the altar, Francesco de' Pazzi brutally murdered Giuliano de' Medici while Lorenzo the Magnificent hid from the conspirators in the sacristy. Forty years earlier, the concluding session of the Council of Ferrara-Florence was held here;

it culminated in the signing of the Union Decree, which proclaimed the union of most existing Christian churches (mainly Catholic and Orthodox) into a single structure under the pope. (It was later rejected by the Grand Duke of Moscow and most Byzantine clergy, effectively nullifying the council's achievements.) Fiery preacher Girolamo Savonarola delivered his sermons here, and the first public readings of Dante Alighieri's "Divine Comedy" took place here. A fresco of Dante illuminates Florence on the north nave (left of the entrance).

If you turn around and look above the main entrance, you will see unique clocks showing "Hora Italica" or "Italian Time." Their dial is divided into 24 hours, and the hand moves in the opposite direction from what we are used to. The clock's peculiarity doesn't end there: It reaches its 24th hour not at midnight but at sunset. Thus, it requires constant adjustment as sunset times change throughout the year. This task is managed by two employees of the Museo dell'Opera del Duomo. The original clocks (not exactly these but similar) were constructed and installed in the cathedral by Florentine clockmaker Angelo de Niccolò in 1443. Their mechanism was connected to the bells in Giotto's campanile; when the hand reached the 24th hour, the bells rang, calling Florentines and peasants working in the fields outside the city walls to evening prayer and signaling the imminent closing of the city gates. Today, the clocks are still connected to the campanile bells, but of course, the city gates are no longer closed. The original clocks were replaced by a standard 12-hour clock in 1761, and by the late 18th century, Italy had adopted the modern time system under Napoleon Bonaparte's decree. The original mechanism was restored only in 1973. During restoration, a fresco by Paolo Uccello was discovered under a layer of paint; you can now see it around the clock. At that time, the renowned Florentine watchmaking house Officine Panerai (one of the oldest in the city, with its historic shop and museum located directly across from the baptistery on Piazza del Duomo) was commissioned to restore the original Hora Italica mechanism.

The Baptistery of Saint John

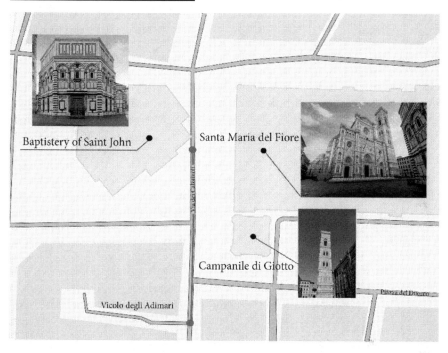

The eminent German architect Adolf von Hildebrand was outraged when, in the 19th century, the city authorities decided to expand the Piazza del Duomo and remove some buildings behind the Baptistery of Saint John. This decision disrupted the original architectural ensemble formed by the Baptistery, the cathedral, and Giotto's Campanile. "Now the Baptistery looks like a misplaced cabinet. It has become meaningless: it is encountered as an obstacle, and the immediate impression of the Cathedral is destroyed," von Hildebrand wrote. Well, we won't be so critical; at least now we have the opportunity to thoroughly inspect this architectural masterpiece from all sides.

To this day, it is not definitively known what stood on the site of the Baptistery in ancient Roman times. Until the 19th century, the theory that a Temple of Mars was located here enjoyed support. However, later archaeological evidence disproved this theory, as under the Baptistery of Saint John was found not a temple but, rather, the remains of an ancient Roman house with a beautiful mosaic floor. Nonetheless, by the 9th century, a church dedicated to John the Baptist already stood here, and in 1128, it was officially transformed into a baptistery: a place where newborns and new converts to Christianity were baptized. In the 12th century, long before the Renaissance, the building was clad in marble, and in the 13th century, the marble floor that remains to this day was added. The mosaics inside, also dating from the 1200s, were created in the Proto-Renaissance style that emerged from Byzantine art. The interior mosaic decoration of the dome, one of the latest embellishments of the Baptistery, dates to the 1270s and was likely the work of three masters: Fra Jacopo, Coppo di Marcovaldo, and Cimabue, the latter of whom was one of the principal artists of Florentine Proto-Renaissance painting.

Of course, the most notable adornment of the Baptistery is the golden "Gates of Paradise" by the eminent Lorenzo Ghiberti, installed on the building's eastern exit in 1452. They are one of three bronze doors of the Baptistery of Saint John, along with the southern doors by Andrea Pisano and the northern ones, also by Ghiberti. The exquisitely crafted panels of the "Gates of Paradise" depict scenes from the Old Testament. Most are framed by rectangular and circular borders with images of biblical figures and prophets. The exception is on the left door, about eye level, in the third-round frame from the bottom. There, you'll find a self-portrait of Lorenzo Ghiberti. This marks one of the Renaissance's revolutionary innovations: individualizing works and creating a "personal brand," as we would say today. We all know that Giotto designed the campanile of Santa Maria del Fiore, but try to recall, for instance, the names of the architects of Hagia Sophia in Constantinople (Istanbul), built 800 years before the Renaissance began.

On either side of the "Gates of Paradise" stand the porphyry "Saracen Columns," a gift from Pisa, given in gratitude for Florence's military assistance in 1117 during Pisa's war with Lucca. At that time, most of Pisa's forces were engaged in battles against the Saracens (Arabs) in the Balearic Islands. Initially, these two columns were placed in the square without any base. However, after they fell and shattered into many pieces, the decision was made to position them against the Baptistery walls.

Other noteworthy, though often overlooked, features of the Baptistery are the two rectangular marks on the southern columns. These are the gold standards of two medieval units of measure used in Florence. The larger one is known as the "Langobard Foot" or "Foot of Liutprand" (named after the Lombard king who reigned from 712 to 744). It's uncertain whether the actual foot length of the ancient king served as the basis for this measure, but the name stuck. The smaller measure is called the "Florentine Measure." According to the most likely hypothesis, these standards were used for brick-making. Farther along, on the same southern side, the base of the Baptistery incorporates a piece of an ancient Roman sarcophagus depicting a ship loading wine barrels after a grape harvest. Most likely, the original owner of the sarcophagus was a wine merchant. Indeed, the reuse of ruined ancient monuments was common practice in the early Middle Ages. This tradition is especially evident in Byzantine and early Christian architecture in Athens, for which your humble servant has also written an excellent guide.

Palazzo Martelli (Casa Martelli)

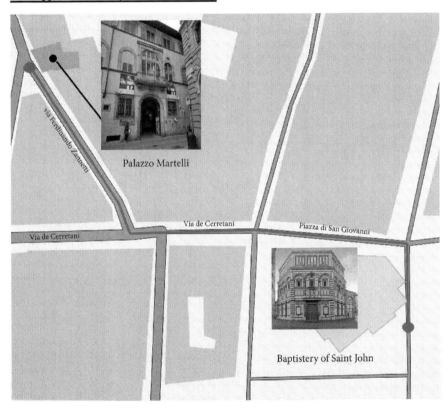

Palazzo Martelli

Baptistery of Saint John

Continuing our journey through Dante's city, I suggest we leave Piazza del Duomo via Via de' Cerretani. After a short walk, turn right onto Via Ferdinando Zannetti. This street is named after the Italian surgeon and revolutionary Ferdinando Zannetti, who lived on a nearby street. He became famous in 1862 for performing a complex and successful operation to remove a bullet from the leg of the legendary General Garibaldi. In the process, the surgeon prevented the national hero of Italy from losing his leg.

Soon, Via Ferdinando Zannetti merges with Via dei Conti. At the junction, under number 8, stands one of Florence's notable mansions, Palazzo Martelli. Along with Palazzo Davanzati, Orsanmichele, the Medici Chapel, and the National Museum of Bargello, Palazzo Martelli is part of a single museum system. A combined ticket for all five sites can be purchased on the official Musei del Bargello website for €21.

The noble Martelli family owned several houses on this street as early as the beginning of the 16th century. In 1627, these were unified into a single palace after Senator Marco Martelli married his cousin from another branch of the family. The Martelli family were long-time supporters of the Medici, and one of their members, Camilla, became the second wife of Cosimo I, the first Grand Duke of Tuscany, in 1570. This marriage helped rehabilitate other Martelli family members who, because they were suspected of involvement in the Pucci conspiracy, had been exiled from Florence not long before. (We will discuss this matter in more detail later when we reach the main building of the Bargello Museum.)

The Martelli family thrived and, over three centuries, became one of the city's most influential families, amassing rich art collections, mainly paintings. However, in the second half of the 19th century, radical changes occurred in the life of the ancient Tuscan aristocracy. Many families struggled to adapt to new social conditions, leading to a gradual decline in their economic situation. Finding no other means of survival, families like the Martelli began to sell their art collections. Today, individual portraits of the family members can be found in places like the National Gallery of Washington.

The long history of this noble dynasty ended in 1986 with the death of Francesca Martelli, the last owner of the mansion. With no heirs, she bequeathed the family palazzo, along with the remaining artworks, to the Florentine Curia. As it turned out, this decision significantly harmed the Martelli legacy. For the 12 years during which the palazzo was under church management, numerous everyday items (ceramics, dishes, clothing, furniture elements) disappeared without a trace, and due to the lack of inventories, it is impossible to even approximately estimate the extent of these losses. Nonetheless, in 1998, the Curia sold Palazzo Martelli to the Italian government, and after long and meticulous restoration work, the mansion opened its doors to visitors as a museum in 2009. Today, you can see works by outstanding masters such as Pieter Brueghel the Younger, Piero di Cosimo, Salvator Rosa, Luca Giordano, and many others. Of particular interest are the thematic frescoes on the palace walls, such as the "Winter Garden," or the panoramic decorations of the bathroom.

Basilica di San Lorenzo and Cappelle Medicee

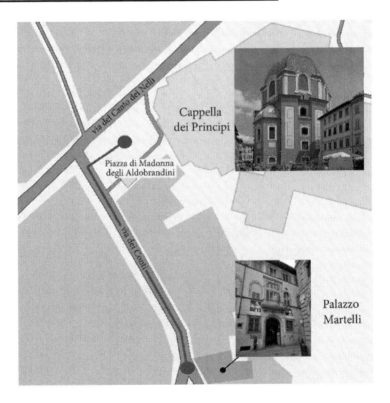

Continuing along Via dei Conti, we will soon arrive at Piazza di Madonna degli Aldobrandini. On our right, we will find the grand Basilica of San Lorenzo (Basilica di San Lorenzo). More precisely, we will see part of the basilica known as the Chapel of the Princes (Cappella dei Principi)—a structure boasting the second-largest dome in Florence after Santa Maria del Fiore. Like Orsanmichele and Palazzo Martelli, the Medici Chapels are part of the Bargello Museum organization. Tickets can be booked on the same website, bargellomusei.it.

If we walk around the basilica and reach Piazza di San Lorenzo, we will find ourselves in front of the main entrance to this church—one of the oldest in Florence. Besides the beautiful monument to Giovanni delle Bande Nere ("Giovanni of the Black Bands"), who was the father of Grand Duke Cosimo I de' Medici, we will immediately notice something unusual about the facade of this majestic basilica. Yes, indeed, it is completely unadorned and, moreover, unfinished. In 1518, when Michelangelo created a wooden model of the facade and was preparing to make his project a reality at the request of Pope Leo X (Giovanni de' Medici), a serious lack of funds was discovered. As a result, the master moved on to other works, and the issue of the facade was revisited only in 2011. At that time, the mayor of Florence, Matteo Renzi, proposed completing the facade by 2015, but this required a national referendum. The matter of holding such a referendum remained unresolved. This was perhaps for the best, as Michelangelo is long gone, and who else could be trusted with such a significant task?

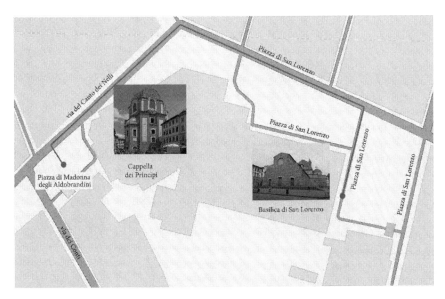

Entering the basilica, you step into an exquisitely detailed and refined interior one that appears to have been crafted by masters of High Classicism in the 18th and 19th centuries. The craftsmanship of the church's decor belies the fact that most of the completed almost 600 years ago. In the right nave, you will find the masterpiece "Marriage of the Virgin" by the painter Rosso Fiorentino. This painting was revolutionary for its time, as Joseph is depicted not as an old man, as was traditional according to the biblical narrative, but as a young man, the same age as Mary. It is believed that the artist reflected the renewal of the Catholic Church in his work. (The early 16th century marked the beginning of the Reformation.)

At the edge of the colonnade dividing the three naves of the basilica, you can see two intriguing bronze pulpits, each mounted on four columns. These are the last creations of the great Donatello. It is likely that the master originally conceived of these elegant works not as church pulpits but as sarcophagi for members of the Medici house (according to the most common theory, for Cosimo the Elder and his wife, Contessina). Exactly how they were transformed into pulpits remains unknown, but they found their place here in the basilica, mounted on columns of dark marble, in 1515, during a visit to Florence by Pope Leo X.

Michelangelo Buonarroti. Attributed to Daniele da Volterra (1509–1566).

On the left side is the entrance to the Old Sacristy (Sagrestia Vecchia), a room designed by Filippo Brunelleschi and decorated by Donatello. Here, you can see the sarcophagi of Giovanni di Bicci de' Medici, who founded the illustrious dynasty of Florentine rulers and patrons of great art, as well as of his wife, Piccarda, and two of their descendants: the banker Giovanni and the de facto ruler of Florence, Piero "the Gouty."

Opposite the Old Sacristy is the New Sacristy—another masterpiece by Michelangelo. When you enter, you might not be impressed at first. Yes, the view might seem less grandiose, especially after the architectural and sculptural marvels we have already seen. Certainly, it is modest in size. However, Michelangelo, the great master of stone, imbued this space with an extraordinary sense of harmony. The master began work on it in 1520, commissioned by Pope Leo X and his relative, Cardinal Giulio de' Medici (the future Pope Clement VII). The commission arose from the sudden deaths of two important family members: Giuliano, Duke of Nemours, who was supposed to receive the crown of Naples (1516), and Lorenzo, Duke of Urbino and ruler of Florence (1519). This chapel was to be their resting place, and their sarcophagi are what we see here now. Above the tombs sit the marble Medici figures—the very same Dukes Giuliano and Lorenzo (in a helmet). Their sarcophagi are topped with allegorical sculptures: Dusk and Dawn (Lorenzo's tomb) and Day and Night (Giuliano's tomb). Michelangelo intended to sculpt four more allegorical figures representing rivers; these were to lie at the foot of the tombs. However, in 1527, the Medici family was expelled from Florence, and work halted.

These sculptures collectively set the main philosophical theme for the entire space as a unified work of art: mourning the swift passage of time, the sorrow of fleeting youth, the sadness of the impossibility of turning back time, just as one cannot make a river change its course. This thought more deeply permeates you the longer you stand here and observe these curves of cold stone in unnatural poses, in sorrow, in sadness, lying through the tension of every part of the bodies on the lids of the coffins of those whose very bones no longer remain.

As for Michelangelo, a staunch supporter of the Republic who nevertheless enjoyed the patronage of the Medici, he joined the rebels after the powerful family was expelled from Florence. He was appointed chief inspector of the city's fortifications. In 1530, when Florence was besieged by the forces of Emperor Charles V, who acted in alliance with the Medici, Michelangelo was one of the leaders of the city's defense as an engineer and mechanic. However, his genius alone was not enough, and Florence fell to the enemy. Fearing retribution from his former patrons, the great artist took refuge in the Basilica of San Lorenzo, where he had previously worked, in a hidden room of about 30 square meters, accessible from the New Sacristy. Throughout August and September 1530, Michelangelo lived unnoticed in this secret room, where he left numerous charcoal sketches on the walls. These sketches remained unknown even after Michelangelo fled to Venice in September 1530 and after his return to Florence at the request of Pope Clement VII (Giulio de' Medici) to complete his work on the New Sacristy. This room was discovered by chance in 1975 during a search for an alternative entrance to the chapel. Not until November 2023 was it opened to the public under limited visitation conditions. Only four people can enter every 15 minutes, so it is advisable to book tickets to Michelangelo's secret room in advance.

The third chapel in the Basilica of San Lorenzo, which we have already seen from the outside, i.e., the "Chapel of the Princes," is situated between the Old and New Sacristies. This space is notable because it was designed by Don Giovanni de' Medici, the illegitimate son of Cosimo I, Grand Duke of Tuscany. Together with sculptor Matteo Nigetti, he began work on this chapel in 1604. This magnificent work of architectural art took nearly 360 years to complete. While most of the work was finished by the mid-18th century, the inlaying of the floor with precious stones was completed only in 1962. Thus, the Chapel of the Princes, commissioned by Ferdinando I de' Medici, was completed 200 years after the end of the grand ducal dynasty itself. (Its last representative was Anna Maria Luisa de' Medici, who died in 1743.) And, yes, these luxurious tombs are actually empty, although they bear the names of six Tuscan rulers: Cosimo I, Ferdinando I, Cosimo II, Francesco I, Ferdinando II, and Cosimo III. Their remains rest not here but beneath the basilica, in the crypt where other members of the illustrious dynasty are interred.

Palazzo Medici Riccardi

Adjacent to Piazza di San Lorenzo, on via de' Gori, lies another significant landmark: the Palazzo Medici Riccardi and its adjoining garden. The land for this garden was once acquired by Clarice Orsini, wife of Lorenzo the Magnificent and mother of Pope Leo X. It was here where the young Michelangelo Buonarroti began to hone his craft, copying beautiful ancient sculptures. He was one of many students at Florence's first art academy, which operated under the patronage of the Medici and was led by Bertoldo di Giovanni, a pupil of Donatello. Thus, Michelangelo indirectly inherited Donatello's expertise. This connection was no secret: Michelangelo's "David" was significantly influenced by his illustrious predecessor's bronze "David," which also resided here in the Palazzo Medici until the time of Savonarola.

Cosimo de' Medici the Elder commissioned this massive and imposing building to mark his new, high position in Florence after his return from exile in 1434. Renowned architect Filippo Brunelleschi competed for the position of chief architect of the future Medici residence. However, his design seemed too grandiose to Cosimo the Elder, who wanted to avoid public and aristocratic dissent. Instead, the patriarch of the future Tuscan ducal dynasty appointed Michelozzo di Bartolomeo as the chief architect.

Florence experienced turbulent times during the 15th and 16th centuries, so the palace was designed with powerful, rough, almost fortress-like walls (like most other noble palazzi in Florence) and with the intention that its owners wouldn't need to leave its premises. The palace included a spacious courtyard that housed sculptures (including Donatello's "David"), fruit trees, and benches. Similar courtyards, surrounded by "arcades on columns" (peristyles), were a signature of Michelozzo's work in many buildings he was commissioned to design. This led Florentines to call them "Michelozzo's courtyards."

The palazzo was completed in 1460. By 1492, when the Medici were expelled from the city and Girolamo Savonarola became the de facto dictator of Florence, the residence had been looted, and many artworks were auctioned off at Orsanmichele. During this time, Donatello's "David" moved to Palazzo Vecchio, and his sculpture "Judith and Holofernes" moved to Piazza della Signoria. The palace's troubles didn't end there; the Medici returned to the city, but in 1527, they were again expelled, and their main urban residence was once again plundered. It was restored in 1530 after the family's return to the city. For seven years thereafter, it was owned by the Duke of Florence, Alessandro de' Medici, who was murdered by his cousin Lorenzino for unclear reasons. Alessandro's successor, Cosimo I from the junior branch of the Medici dynasty, chose Palazzo Vecchio as his residence, leaving this palace to house the youngest members of the family until the mid-17th century. The palace acquired its double name after Grand Duke of Tuscany Ferdinand II de' Medici sold it to the prosperous Riccardi family, who held the title of marquises. Out of respect for the Medici legacy, these last private owners did not significantly alter the interiors or exterior. In 1814, the Riccardi sold the palazzo to the Tuscan government, which established its residence there 60 years later. Along with the palazzo, the Riccardi handed over their excellent library, which had been publicly accessible since 1715. Today, this luxurious collection of rare books (such as manuscripts by Niccolò Machiavelli and a 10th-century copy of Pliny's "Natural History") belongs to the Accademia della Crusca, one of the main institutions regulating the norms of the Italian literary language.

Detail of a fresco by Benozzo Gozzoli, which, according to a popular version, depicts the Byzantine Emperor John Palaeologus as the "middle magus."

Undoubtedly, the most impressive room in Palazzo Medici Riccardi is the Chapel of the Magi, which Benozzo Gozzoli painted in 1461. The frescoes in this chapel are remarkable for two reasons. First, when you enter it, you witness an opulent spectacle: Nobles dressed in silks and capes embroidered with gold, accompanied by large retinues, ride on pedigreed horses with precious harnesses along a picturesque road in the Tuscan hills, following a caravan of gift-laden camels. You can't help but sense a subtle irony here, as the fresco is titled "The Procession of the Magi," and the Magi—Caspar, Balthazar, and Melchior—who brought their gifts to the stable where the Messiah was born under the star, are typically depicted much more modestly. This is the second reason why the chapel's frescoes attract attention. Of course, there are excellently carved benches with plant motifs and coats of arms, as well as a wonderful marble floor, but don't be distracted by this visual noise; we are here for more than furniture and stones, of which there are plenty in Florence! If we divide this narrative into three parts, as Gozzoli did, starting to "read" the image from the eastern side of the chapel (which will be on your right if you stand facing the altar), we will see that the first prominent figure is a young man with golden curls, sitting on a white horse whose harness is richly decorated with gold embroidery and Medici coats of arms. This youth is usually identified as Lorenzo "the Magnificent," the future ruler of Florence, who was 12 years old at the time of the fresco's creation in 1461. Note his headgear: a golden crown with equal triangular spikes adorned with precious stones. In European heraldry, this type of crown is known as the "Eastern Crown," and it is traditionally depicted on the heads of ancient Eastern rulers, such as Cyrus the Great, Seleucus Nicator, and the Egyptian Pharaohs of the Ptolemaic dynasty. In this case, the crown indicates Lorenzo's role in the procession: that of one of the Magi or Eastern Kings, as they are called in the Catholic tradition. Thus, Lorenzo personifies the "Young King"—Caspar. This "Eastern Crown" also helps us identify the "Middle-aged King"—Balthazar. Following "Caspar" Lorenzo, also on horseback, are other members of the dynasty: Piero de' Medici, ruler of Florence from 1464-1469 (riding a white horse with a harness adorned with the motto "Semper"—"Always") and behind him, also in a red cap, according to popular belief, his father and Lorenzo's grandfather, Cosimo de' Medici the Elder, who ruled Florence from 1434-1464 and was still alive at the time of the fresco's creation. As we recall from our visit to the Cathedral of Santa Maria del Fiore, during Cosimo the Elder's rule, Florence hosted the Ecumenical Council of Christian Churches, aiming to sign the decree of union between the Orthodox Constantinople Patriarchate and the Catholic Rome. In 1439, a large Greek delegation led by Byzantine Emperor John VIII Palaiologos and the Patriarch of Constantinople, Joseph II, visited Florence. Benozzo Gozzoli witnessed their stay in the city, which likely inspired this fresco, and he even depicted himself among the Greek guests. We can find him by the red cap with the golden inscription "Opus Benotii"—"Work of Benozzo." To his left is an elderly man—George Gemistos Plethon, a Byzantine philosopher and close friend of the Byzantine emperors. Directly above Plethon, in a red hat, is Cardinal Enea Silvio Bartolomeo Piccolomini—a prominent humanist, writer, poet, historian, and future Pope Pius II. To his left, slightly behind the cardinal, is Catholic Cardinal and Patriarch of Kyiv Isidore, also a great humanist with a remarkable destiny. We won't turn our acquaintance with the fresco into a full-fledged history lecture, but these details will help us further "read" the work's narrative, especially when we identify Balthazar—the second of the Three Kings. He is the man in gold-embroidered garments, with golden curls, a beard, a mustache, and upward-gazing blue eyes, possibly with a slight squint—a feature considered a sign of regal beauty in those times and frequently found in Renaissance frescoes, paintings, and sculptures. Who is this person representing Balthazar? According to the most common version, it is the same Byzantine Emperor John VIII Palaiologos (1392-1448), who strived to save his country from the Muslim Turks' onslaught by forming a church-political alliance with Catholic Europe. In 1439, in Florence, Emperor John VIII and Pope Eugene IV solemnly opened the Ecumenical Council, which, as mentioned earlier, signed the decree uniting the Catholic and Orthodox churches under the pope's supremacy over the Patriarch of Constantinople. The fact that this move was not accepted by most Byzantine aristocrats and Orthodox clergy significantly contributed to Byzantium's inevitable collapse in 1453. In the corner of the same wall, we also see three more members of the Medici family: Lorenzo "the Magnificent"'s sisters Maria, Bianca, and Lucrezia, dressed in male clothing and riding horses.

Moving to the third wall, the third "chapter" of Gozzoli's narrative, we again encounter his self-portrait. This time, it is not among Greek philosophers and humanists; rather, it is among Florentine patricians and bankers. Here he is, turning toward us in his azure hood with a white handkerchief, while the banker Francesco Sassetti, standing to his right, shows us his palm. As for the next figure (a young man in a blue tunic, sitting on a horse with a small leopard on a beautiful leash), there is no consensus. Some researchers believe Gozzoli depicted Thomas Palaiologos, the younger brother of Emperor John VIII, who was living in Rome at the time of the fresco's creation and was recognized as the Byzantine Emperor in exile, as the Turks had already captured Constantinople. Other art historians see this young man as Castruccio Castracani (1281-1328), a condottiero and Duke of Lucca, the hero of Niccolò Machiavelli's "Life of Castruccio Castracani."

The concluding figure of the procession is the "Old King Melchior"— an elderly man with a gray beard, his head crowned with the same "Eastern Crown," depicted, like the other two "Kings".

Accademia Gallery of Florence and Medici Museum

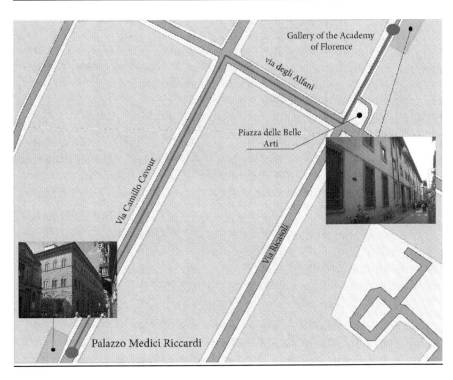

It is very easy to get from the Palazzo Medici to the Accademia Gallery. In this great city, everything is unexpectedly close together— the ceilings painted by Michelangelo, the floors trodden by Dante, and the Medici tombs beneath them.

We'll take Via Camillo Cavour to the intersection with Via degli Alfani. From there, we'll walk to Piazza delle Belle Arti—Square of the Fine Arts. Via Ricasoli, which leads out from the square, will take us directly to the Accademia Gallery, one of Florence's main museums. Undoubtedly, its most important exhibit is the original "David" by Michelangelo, which was moved here in 1872 from Piazza della Signoria. In addition to this masterpiece, you will find works by outstanding Renaissance artists such as Domenico Ghirlandaio, Fra Filippo Lippi, Sandro Botticelli, Giotto, and others. The extensive collection of Russian icons, which the Accademia

Gallery housed until 2021, is now displayed on the first floor of the Palazzo Pitti.

This guide will not dwell too much on the exhibits of this museum, as I want you, dear reader, to be able to carry it without a cart. However, if you are interested in learning something unusual about the works of art in Florence's galleries, something no other guidebook or tour guide will tell you, you can contact me on Facebook or Instagram or via the email listed at the end of the book. If there is enough interest, I will release a separate guide to Florence's museums.

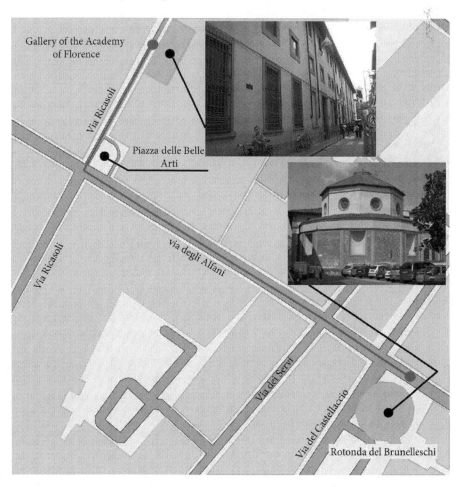

For now, I invite you to continue along Via degli Alfani until you come upon an octagonal rotunda with empty niches and a tiled roof.

This is the "Brunelleschi Rotunda," a structure on which the great architect worked simultaneously with the dome of Santa Maria del Fiore. The funds for constructing this rotunda, originally intended to be a church dedicated to the Virgin Mary and the Twelve Apostles, were bequeathed to Florence by one of its distinguished sons, the military commander Filippo Scolari (also known as Pippo Spano). Scolari gained fame as a general in the service of the King of Hungary and Emperor Sigismund I of the Holy Roman Empire during the wars with the Turks. Five thousand gold florins from his estate were given to the Florentine wool merchants' guild, which then commissioned Brunelleschi to build the church. However, the architect could not complete the work; when the walls of the future church were already constructed, the government confiscated the remaining funds from Scolari's legacy to cover the expenses of the war with the neighboring Republic of Lucca. Ultimately, the rotunda was not finished until the 17th century. It now forms part of the Medici Museum, which opened in 2019 to mark the 500th anniversary of the birth of Cosimo I, Grand Duke of Tuscany. This museum houses a collection of personal items and artworks from the private collection of the Medici family, along with documents and multimedia installations that provide insight into the history of the renowned dynasty of ruthless tyrants and generous patrons of artists and sculptors.

Spedale degli Innocenti and Piazza della Santissima Annunziata

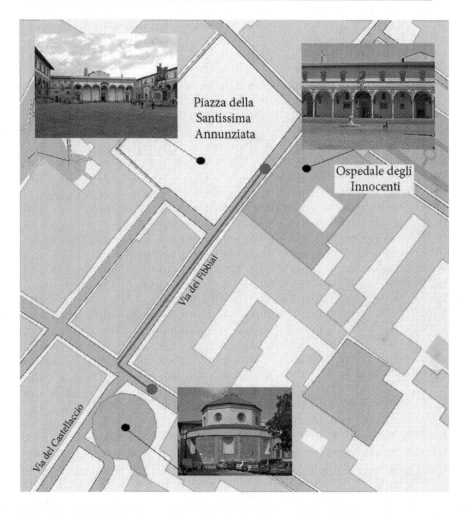

Via dei Fibbiai leads us from the Brunelleschi Rotunda to Piazza della Santissima Annunziata—another significant spot in Florence that tourists sometimes overlook. Here, alongside two fountains adorned with sea monsters by Pietro Tacca and his joint creation with Giambologna, the equestrian statue of Grand Duke Ferdinando I de' Medici, stands a very important structure: the "House of the Innocents" or "Ospedale degli Innocenti" by Filippo Brunelleschi. This is one of the first buildings of the Italian Renaissance, and it set the tone for an entire architectural era. The long building with a loggia will be on your right as soon as you step into the square. The Florentine silk merchants' guild commissioned Filippo Brunelleschi to design this building in 1419, and over the next eight years, he oversaw its construction according to his plans. With only minor deviations from the original design, the building was completed in 1445 and became the first orphanage of such scale in Europe.

Just ten days after the orphanage opened—on February 10, 1445—the first foundling arrived. (A special window, used to anonymously leave a baby at the orphanage, was built in 1660 and remains intact in the orphanage's loggia.) By tradition, foundlings in Florence were typically given the surnames Degl'Innocenti or Nocentini ("of the Innocents" and "Innocent"). These names are still common among Florentines and their descendants worldwide. Not until the 19th century was this tradition replaced by the practice of naming children after saints commemorated on the day when the orphanage staff found them at the special window.

Brunelleschi's architectural solutions embodied in this building (such as the arcade supported by columns—the most prominent part of the facade) set the tone for the later stylistics of the Italian Renaissance.

Although the old orphanage closed in 1875, it still houses charities related to childhood and motherhood and UNICEF offices, known as the Istituto degli Innocenti. Additionally, the Brunelleschi masterpiece hosts the Spedale degli Innocenti Museum. Detailed information is available in the "Museums" section at the end of this book.

On the opposite side of the square is the Loggia dei Serviti, the "counterpart" to Brunelleschi's "House of the Innocents." It was constructed in the 16th century by the Order of the Servants of Mary, a Florentine monastic order founded three centuries earlier and associated with the Basilica of the Santissima Annunziata, a monumental architectural landmark crowning the square. The first church or oratory at this site was established in 1081 during the reign of the notable Margravine Matilda of Tuscany. At that time, and for many years thereafter, this area lay outside Florence's city walls and was primarily farmland. By the 13th century, the ancient oratory had fallen into disrepair. The townspeople appealed to Florentine Bishop Ardinghiero Trotti and seven young men, who had twice experienced visions of a weeping Virgin Mary, to restore the oratory. Thus, in 1233, the Order of the Servants of Mary was founded, and in 1250, its members laid the cornerstone of the future basilica on the site of the old oratory. The construction and embellishment of the main basilica building and its numerous chapels continued over the centuries. Today, the basilica still functions as a church, while the Loggia dei Serviti, acquired in the mid-19th century by the Budini Gattai family (who also own the adjacent three-story palazzo), has housed the Hotel Loggiato dei Serviti for the past 150 years. (Detailed information can be found in the relevant section of this guidebook.)

A bit farther along via Gino Capponi lies the Palazzo della Crocetta, built in the 17th century for Maria Maddalena de' Medici, sister of the Grand Duke of Tuscany, Cosimo II. Born with very short legs and suffering from various other congenital ailments throughout her brief life of 33 years, the princess lived as a recluse in her residence. To allow Maria Maddalena to attend religious services without attracting unwanted attention from the townspeople, the palace architect, Giulio Parigi, connected the residence to the Basilica of the Santissima Annunziata via covered overhead galleries. However, shortly after the princess's death, these galleries were demolished, and the palace was separated from the monastery. It became a private residence that changed hands several times over the following centuries. After the unification of Italy and the proclamation of Florence as the capital, the Palazzo della Crocetta housed the Royal Audit Office. In 1880, it was converted to accommodate the collection of the Florence Archaeological Museum, which remains there to this day. The museum offers a wealth of intriguing artifacts from Etruscan, ancient Roman, ancient Greek, and ancient Egyptian art, including a female portrait from the famous necropolis in Al-Fayoum and reliefs from the tombs of pharaohs of the 18th and 19th dynasties (14th and 13th centuries BC).

Palazzo Pazzi and Museo Nazionale del Bargello

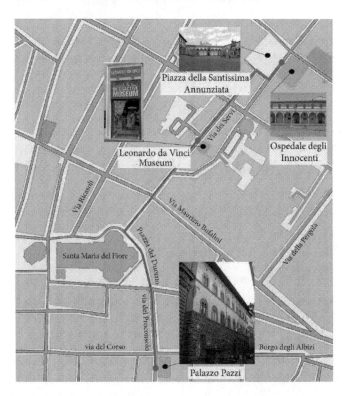

Via dei Servi, named after the Order of the Servants of Mary, leads us from Piazza della Santissima Annunziata directly back to Piazza del Duomo, where the Cathedral of Santa Maria del Fiore stands. Along this street, you'll find the intriguing Leonardo da Vinci Museum, where many of the inventions of the great Tuscan scientist and artist have been recreated, allowing visitors to explore the principles behind these creations.

From the square, we head down via del Proconsolo, passing the intersection with via del Corso and Borgo degli Albizi, until we reach Palazzo Pazzi—one of the Florentine residences of the Pazzi family, known for their failed conspiracy against Lorenzo the Magnificent. The current building was constructed on the foundations of two older mansions that the Pazzi family purchased in 1476, shortly before their expulsion from the city following the failed plot against the Medici. The houses were transferred to the loyal Medici family, the Gherardini della Rosa, from whom the Pazzi repurchased them in the 16th century upon their return to Florence. It was during this time that the palazzo acquired its present appearance.

In 1735, a small, tower-like structure in the palazzo, resembling a dovecote but offering an excellent view of Florence, officially became home to the "Accademia La Colombaria"—the "Dovecote Academy." This society of scholarly friends, founded by the palace's owner, Giovanni Girolamo de' Pazzi, included notable figures such as physicist and astronomer Ruggero Giuseppe Boscovich, future Naples State Secretary Bernardo Tanucci, theologian and bibliophile Angelo Maria Bandini, and economist Ferdinando Galiani.

Throughout the 19th century, the Pazzi-founded Academy focused solely on the study of Tuscan history. During the Fascist regime in Italy and especially during the retreat of Nazi German troops, the Academy, which then occupied the entire palazzo, suffered significant damage, with much of its library and furniture destroyed. Nevertheless, after the war, the Academy resumed its activities as the Tuscan Academy of Sciences and Letters, "La Colombaria." Today, it is divided into four classes: Philology and Literary Criticism;

Historical and Philosophical Sciences; Legal, Economic, and Social Sciences; and Physical, Mathematical, and Natural Sciences.

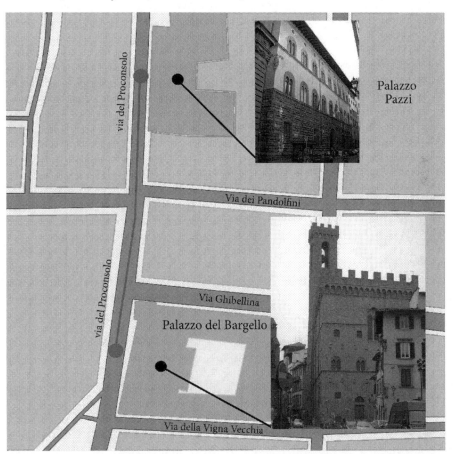

Continuing along via del Proconsolo, we arrive at the main building of the Bargello Museum, one of the three most significant museums in Florence, alongside the Accademia Gallery and the Uffizi Gallery. We have already visited some of the Bargello Museum's branches (the Medici Chapel, Orsanmichele, and Palazzo Martelli). Here, in the Bargello Palace itself, the most valuable works of Florentine Renaissance sculpture are exhibited, including Donatello's "David" and "Saint George," Michelangelo's "Bacchus," and many others. In this museum, you can also see the original right panel of the famous "Franks Casket"—a fine piece of 8th-century Anglo-Saxon art, richly decorated with Old English runes and mythological scenes. The Bargello Museum purchased it in the late 19th century.

The name of the palace, which was later transferred to the museum, originates from the ancient Germanic word "burg," meaning "fortress," which evolved into the Late Latin term "bargillus" (via the Gothic "bargi") and then into the Italian language. Indeed, built in the mid-13th century in the Italian Gothic style, the palace resembles a classic castle. However, the Florentines did not initially associate the word "Bargello" with architecture; for many centuries, it referred to the head of the city militia, who safeguarded Florence "like a fortress." Before this name was transferred to the castle before us, the building housed the residence of the elected "Captain of the People" of Florence and, later, the head of the city's magistrate (government)—the podestà. In those times, this palace was known as the "Palazzo del Podestà." As the oldest administrative building in the city, it served as a model for the construction of the Palazzo Vecchio we know today. Not until 1574, after the Medici rulers of Florence abolished the position of the podestà, was the empty palace transformed into the residence of the "Bargello"—the head of the city militia—and thus received its current name.

In the following years, the Bargello Palace was used as a city prison. Until the abolition of the death penalty in the Grand Duchy of Tuscany in 1786, executions were carried out in the castle's inner courtyard. The palace became a museum in 1859, when, amid the wave of revolutions and wars for unification sweeping Italy, the temporary governor of Tuscany declared the deposition of Grand Duke Leopold II and proclaimed the prison in the ancient castle abolished. The museum officially opened in 1865. Since then, it has housed one of the largest collections of Italian Gothic and Renaissance sculpture.

Basilica of the Holy Cross and Pazzi Chapel

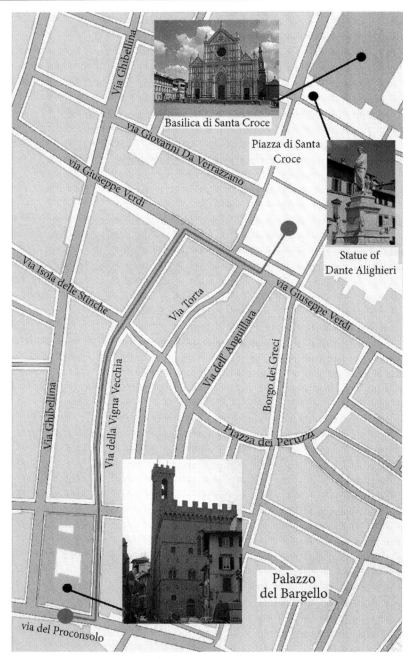

Basilica di Santa Croce

Piazza di Santa Croce

Statue of Dante Alighieri

Palazzo del Bargello

From the Bargello Museum, we will turn onto Via della Vigna Vecchia and proceed to its junction with Via Giuseppe Verdi. Here, we will turn right and soon find ourselves at Piazza di Santa Croce—the Square of the Holy Cross, home to the eponymous basilica, another iconic landmark of Florence.

As we approach, we are greeted by the marble figure of Dante, gazing sternly toward the southern side of the square, surrounded by four Marzocco lions—symbols of Florence—and a "rising from the ashes Roman eagle," as described by the creator of this sculptural composition, Enrico Pazzi (no relation to the infamous dynasty). Behind Dante rises the masterpiece of Florentine Gothic architecture, the basilica itself, which houses the final resting places of the greatest sons of this immortal city: Michelangelo Buonarroti, Niccolò Machiavelli, Leon Battista Alberti, Vittorio Alfieri, and Gioachino Rossini.

There is also room for foreigners, such as the Pisan Galileo Galilei and the Polish composer Prince Michał Kleofas Ogiński. However, Dante Alighieri, the exile, never found peace in his native land; his mausoleum is in Ravenna, while here in Santa Croce, there is only a cenotaph erected in 1829. Interestingly, the inscription on this cenotaph refers to the father of the modern Italian language as a "Tuscan" or "Etruscan."

Michelangelo's lavish tomb was created by Giorgio Vasari, a sculptor and architect who is perhaps even better known for his "Lives of the Most Excellent Painters, Sculptors, and Architects" —the first and only collection of 178 biographies of Italian Renaissance artists at the time, which laid the foundation for modern art history. Perhaps Michelangelo himself would have preferred a much more modest tomb, but, as is well known, true geniuses are usually marked by their humility.

In the chapels of the basilica, you can also find works by early Renaissance artists such as Giotto and another whose name remains a mystery. This artist is identified only by his single known work, the altarpiece of Saint Francis in the Bardi Chapel (located to the right of the church choir)—the "Master of San Francesco Bardi." Giotto adorned the Baroncelli Chapel with his polyptych, "The Coronation of the Virgin". In the Bardi di Vernio Chapel, you can also see Donatello's "Crucifixion". The basilica's cloister, which is part of the Franciscan monastery and the largest Franciscan church in Italy, is home to another architectural masterpiece by Filippo Brunelleschi: the famous Pazzi Chapel.

The creation of the Pazzi Chapel dates back to the first half of the 15th century. In 1423, a fire destroyed the library and part of the residential quarters of the Santa Croce monastery. To restore them, the city authorities announced a competition in which architects and potential sponsors participated. Among them were representatives of the Medici, Spinelli, and Pazzi families. The Pazzi ultimately won. Andrea de' Pazzi, a member of the family, proposed financing the construction of the monastery's chapter house provided that the rear part would serve as the Pazzi family mausoleum. He intended to dedicate it to his heavenly patron, Saint Andrew the Apostle.

Unfortunately, the detailed history of the project and the preparations for construction remain unknown. Nevertheless, in 1441, Filippo Brunelleschi started working on the future Pazzi Chapel; by 1443, Pope Eugene IV was staying there while visiting Florence. The construction was not fully completed until 1478, after Brunelleschi's death. The interior decoration was done by his friend Luca della Robbia, who adorned the chapel's dome with rich paintings featuring the Pazzi family coat of arms, as well as roundels (medallions) depicting scenes from the life of Saint Andrew the Apostle. Additionally, in the dome above the chapel's altar, Brunelleschi, who also had a keen interest in astronomy, depicted the constellations visible in the night sky over Florence on July 4, 1442—the date when work on the chapel resumed after a brief pause due to funding issues.

The founding of the Santa Croce Monastery is traditionally associated with Saint Francis of Assisi, the founder of the monastic order that, in his memory, was named the Franciscan Order. In 1226, a small group of Saint Francis' followers, who preached asceticism and the renunciation of all worldly goods as key Christian virtues, settled near the old city walls of Florence and established an oratory—a prayer house—on the future site of the monastery. In the mid-13th century, this oratory was converted into a full-fledged church, becoming the center of the Franciscan community. As the community grew, the original church became increasingly inadequate for worship services.

Consequently, in 1294, the decision was made to construct a new church. According to the most prevalent version of the story, this task was entrusted to the renowned architect Arnolfo di Cambio. The project was indeed so grand that the primary construction was not completed until 1385. The basilica was consecrated in 1443 by Cardinal Bessarion—a fascinating figure, a Greek from Trebizond (modern-day Trabzon, Turkey), a Byzantine scholar, philosopher, theologian, and humanist, and a major proponent of the union between the Orthodox and Catholic Churches.

Saint Francis of Assisi. Anonymous artist of the Lombard school, mid-17th century.

The basilica suffered significant damage during the flood of November 4-6, 1966—the largest flood in Florence's history. The Arno River rose more than five meters, surpassing the grim record set exactly 633 years earlier by the flood of November 4, 1333. During this deluge, caused by relentless heavy rains across central Italy, the Santa Croce monastic complex bore the brunt of the disaster, as the square on which it stands is one of the lowest points in Florence. Among other losses, the floodwaters destroyed Cimabue's "Crucifixion", created during the Proto-Renaissance period between 1272 and 1280. This artwork, still housed in the Santa Croce Basilica, became a symbol of the devastation wrought by the flood. Other reminders of the two most destructive floods in the city's history are the plaques on Via San Remigio. The first plaque indicates the water level reached in 1333, while the second shows how much higher the floodwaters rose in 1966.

Palazzo Gondi and the Uffizi Gallery

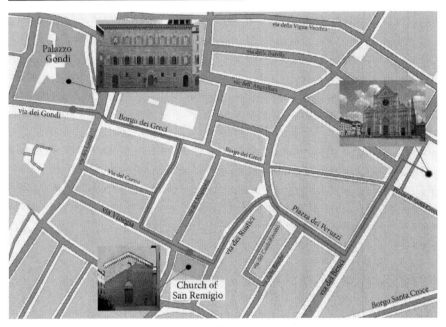

Walking along Via dei Benci, we can turn onto Piazza dei Peruzzi and delve into the web of medieval Florentine streets as we make our way back to Via del Proconsolo. Turning onto the charming Via dei Rustici, we take the first turn onto Via Vinegia and arrive near the Church of San Remigio, on the very street where the two aforementioned plaques commemorate the two most devastating floods in Florence's history. Turning onto Via del Parlagio, we head left onto Borgo dei Greci and arrive at Palazzo Gondi—one of the few Florentine mansions from the Italian Renaissance period still inhabited by the descendants of its original owners, the Gondi family.

This palace is also notable for being built on the site of the former building of the Guild of Cloth Merchants, where the great Leonardo da Vinci resided for a time. It is widely believed that here he painted the portrait of Madonna Lisa Gherardini del Giocondo, the wife of the

Florentine silk merchant Francesco del Giocondo—a rather ordinary portrait of an unremarkable woman by Leonardo's standards but one which, through a series of simple marketing strategies and the creation of a web of remarkably silly myths, now provides considerable annual revenue to the Louvre in Paris. Incidentally, from the window of this building, da Vinci saw Bernardo Bandini, the last participant in the infamous Pazzi Conspiracy, being hanged from the window of Palazzo Vecchio, swinging from a rope.

Later, the house of the Guild was bought by the Florentine patrician Giuliano Gondi, who demolished it to expand his palazzo. Today, a plaque at the entrance to the Gondi family home commemorates this fact: " Leonardo da Vinci spent his happy youth in the house of the Guild of Cloth Merchants, purchased and demolished by Giuliano Gondi to erect this palace, the completion of which in 1874 was marked by a mutual wish of the owner and the city to honor such a glorious name, adorning this elegant and noble building with it."

In other respects, this palazzo is quite typical of its time: The inner courtyard is designed in the style of Michelozzo (similar to what we observed at the Palazzo Medici Riccardi), the ground floor is adorned with rusticated stone (raised stonework), and the windows are fitted with sturdy grilles (as the times were then unsettled). Today, the palace is open for visits by appointment through the official website, and its basement houses a wine bar.

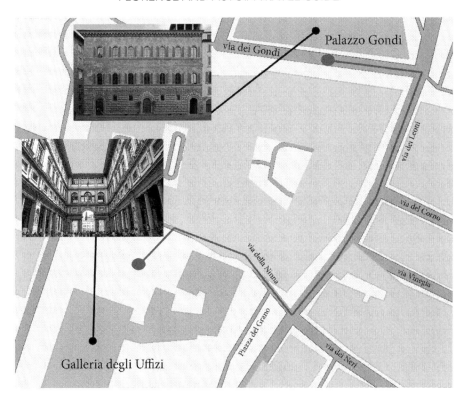

Immediately after Palazzo Gondi, where Via del Proconsolo transitions into Via dei Leoni, you can turn onto the small Via della Ninna and soon find yourself at the entrance to the Uffizi Gallery—the most famous and most visited museum in Italy. This marks the end of our journey along the right bank of the Arno River. We have completed a full circle of its main streets. Now, we will be introduced to the greatest masterpieces of the Italian Renaissance and, of course, the magnificent setting in which they are housed—a technically complex palace created in the 16th century by Giorgio Vasari and situated on the banks of the Arno, built not so much on land but above it.

Originally, the palace housed the offices of the administrative and judicial institutions of the Florentine Magistrate (government). Their consolidation into one building allowed the Grand Duke to better monitor their activities. To enable the Medici family members to move safely between their residence at Palazzo Pitti on the left bank of the Arno and the government buildings, Vasari was assigned an unusual task: to construct a special covered corridor above the city, one that would pass directly over the Ponte Vecchio—the oldest bridge in Florence, located near the present-day Uffizi Gallery. The name "Uffizi" itself indicates the original role of the palace; in Italian, "Uffizi" means "Offices."

Currently, the gallery is fully open to visitors. The exception is the San Pier Scheraggio hall, which consists of the nave of the church of the same name, demolished to make way for the Uffizi Palace. This hall is open only for temporary exhibitions or conferences. As for Vasari's Corridor, it has been under restoration since 2016, and its reopening is still anticipated in 2024. I hope that the next edition of my guidebook to Florence and Tuscany will include it.

Among the most outstanding works of art in the Uffizi Gallery are Giotto's "Madonna d'Ognissanti," one of the first depictions of the Virgin Mary in which the artist departs from the iconographic conventions of the Byzantine tradition to detail the fabric in which she is draped; Leonardo da Vinci's "Annunciation"; the famous "The Birth of Venus" and the stunning "Primavera" by Sandro Botticelli; Michelangelo's "Doni Tondo" (The Holy Family with the Young Saint John the Baptist); and, of course, the incredible "Medusa" by Caravaggio. Additionally, in the Uffizi, you will see numerous ancient sculptures and busts, miniatures, and portraits of prominent Florentines. And don't forget to look around, as the gallery's interior is a work of art in its own right.

Ponte Vecchio (Vecchio Bridge)

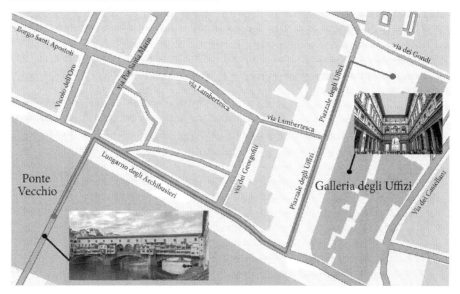

There are cities in this world to which one can't return.

The sun beats on their windows as though on polished mirrors.

And no amount of gold will make their hinged gates turn.

Rivers in those cities always flow beneath six bridges.

There are places in those cities where lips first pressed on lips

And pen on paper. In those cities there's a richness

Of scarecrows cast in iron, of colonnades, arcades.

There the crowds besieging trolley stops are speaking

In the language of a man who's been written off as dead.

This is how one of the great Russian poets of the 20th century, Joseph Brodsky, wrote about Florence (translated from Russian by Maurice English and George L. Kline). The six bridges under which the Arno River eternally flows are actually ten, and the oldest and only one that has remained virtually unchanged since the 16th century is the "Old Bridge"—"Ponte Vecchio." All its neighbors, including the two closest—Santa Trinita Bridge and Ponte alle Grazie—were completely rebuilt after World War II. In 1944, during their retreat from Tuscany, Nazi German troops blew up all the crossings over the Arno except for Ponte Vecchio. The sad fate that befell the Florentine bridges, including the Ponte alle Grazie, built in the 13th century and over a hundred years older than Ponte Vecchio, did not assail Italy's most famous bridge thanks to the German consul in Florence, Gerhard Wolf (1896-1971), a Bavarian-born lawyer and diplomat appointed to his post in 1940. During the German army's retreat from the city, Wolf managed to convince the Wehrmacht command that the "Vasari Corridor" running over Ponte Vecchio had no strategic value. Thus, he saved the bridge from destruction. Additionally, during his diplomatic service, Wolf saved several Italian Jews from arrest and deportation to concentration camps. (One of those saved by Wolf, together with the Reich's plenipotentiary minister in Italy, Rudolf

Rahn, was Renaissance art expert Bernard Berenson.) In memory of this man and his role in preserving Florence's cultural heritage during World War II, a commemorative plaque was installed on Ponte Vecchio in 2007.

But what about the bridge itself? At least two earlier bridges likely preceded the current Ponte Vecchio. The first, a Roman bridge, was constructed at the dawn of Florence's history and was expanded and fortified in 123 AD during the reign of Emperor Hadrian. Thus, it became part of the Cassian Way—one of the main routes of the Apennine Peninsula, connecting Etruria (Tuscany) with the city of Rome. This bridge was probably destroyed in the 6th and 7th centuries during the barbarian invasions of Tuscany, and the subsequent fate of crossings over the Arno is difficult to trace. However, it is believed that during the reign of Emperor Charlemagne (who, as we know, stayed in Florence twice), a large wooden bridge was built at the site of Ponte Vecchio; it was fortified in the 9th or 10th century and rebuilt after collapsing in a flood in 1177. This bridge, in turn, was repeatedly damaged by floods and fires but was finally destroyed during one of the largest floods in Florence's history. On November 4, 1333, the water rose 4.22 meters (13.10 feet) above the current level of the Arno, claiming the lives of about 300 Florentines.

After this flood, the current Ponte Vecchio was built. In the 16th century, it was complemented by the famous "Vasari Corridor," connecting the residence of the Grand Dukes of Tuscany in Palazzo Pitti with the government seat of Florence in Palazzo Vecchio. The numerous shops and stores on the "Old Bridge" appeared a bit earlier, in the mid-15th century. At that time, the primary occupants of the bridge were butchers, as the river flowing directly under their shops was convenient for disposing of "production waste." In 1495, the Florence municipality sold the 48 existing shops on Ponte Vecchio to private individuals, trade guilds, and religious organizations, and these new owners began expanding them, primarily through extensions on the exterior. All these numerous and rather chaotic modifications gave the bridge its modern appearance.

The only change to the bridge came in 1938, when, by Mussolini's decree, large panoramic windows were installed in the central part of the Vasari Corridor for Adolf Hitler's visit to Florence.

Today, two plaques commemorate the bridge's complex history. Both recount how the "Ponte Vecchio" was destroyed by the flood on November 4, 1333, and then rebuilt with even greater beauty and elegance. One of these plaques is located near a building just before the monument to the renowned Mannerist master, sculptor, and architect Benvenuto Cellini (if you are coming from the Uffizi Gallery). This plaque is the least well-preserved and is difficult to read. However, on the opposite side, under the arches of the Vasari Corridor, is an obelisk with a much clearer inscription: "On November 4, 1333, this bridge collapsed due to the swirl of many waters; then in 1345, it was rebuilt, more beautiful and elegant. This child briefly shows what happened." Indeed, on the right side of the 14th-century plaque, we see the image of a winged infant, but what exactly it signifies and what it wants to show us remains unclear.

Palazzo Pitti and the Boboli Gardens

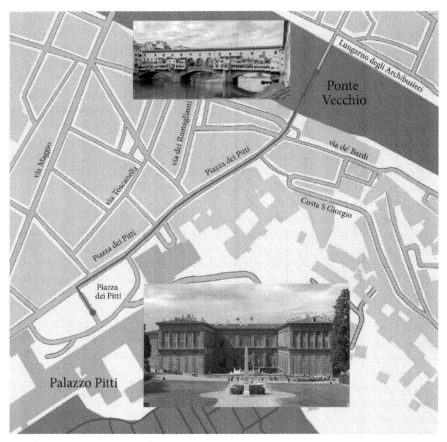

Our final stop in the wonderful city of Florence is the main residence of the Grand Dukes of Tuscany and one of the largest museum complexes in Florence—the Palazzo Pitti. This is where the famous Vasari Corridor ends, and you can reach it on foot via the Piazza de' Pitti, which starts right from the Ponte Vecchio.

This palace, austere and somewhat rough in appearance, was commissioned by Luca Pitti, a Florentine banker knighted and lavishly rewarded by the Republic's government during the reign of his friend, Cosimo the Elder de' Medici. Despite this friendship, the Medici and Pitti families couldn't avoid rivalry. Thus, when the first stone of the future palazzo was laid in 1458, Luca Pitti decided that the windows of his residence should be larger than the entrance to the Medici Palace. Naturally, such a large project required cheap labor, which was found among criminals fleeing Florence or enemies of the Medici sentenced to exile. Nevertheless, by 1465, Luca Pitti's funds had run out, and his heirs lived in a partially unfinished residence for some time. In 1549, when the Pitti Bank collapsed, the palazzo was purchased by Grand Duchess Eleanor of Toledo, the wife of the famous Cosimo I. Suffering from tuberculosis, Eleanor found the left bank of the Arno much cleaner and more pleasant for living than the crowded and stuffy old city, and she was undoubtedly right. However, moving to a new residence didn't significantly improve her health or that of some of her children with Grand Duke Cosimo I; two of them died before reaching adulthood. It was here, by the way, that the future Queen of France, Maria de' Medici, daughter of Grand Duke

Francesco I and granddaughter of Cosimo I and Eleanor of Toledo, spent her childhood.

During the 16th to 18th centuries, while the Palazzo Pitti was owned by the Grand Dukes of Tuscany from the House of Medici, the palace and its adjoining territories underwent numerous restorations and additions. In the 18th century, architect Giuseppe Ruggieri added two side wings to the main building in imitation of French royal residences. When the Tuscan crown passed to the Habsburg-Lorraine dynasty, the Palazzo Pitti became the favorite residence of Grand Duke Peter Leopold I, a great reformer and humanist who abolished the death penalty in Tuscany and succeeded his older brother on the throne of the Holy Roman Empire in 1790. His son, Grand Duke Ferdinand III of Tuscany, was forced to leave Florence during Napoleon Bonaparte's advance and abdicate the Tuscan throne. After this, the French army plundered the Palazzo Pitti. Several Renaissance and Mannerist masterpieces in its collection, such as Annibale Carracci's "Holy Family," Paolo Veronese's "Moses Crossing the Nile"

Cosimo I de' Medici, Grand Duke of Tuscany (1519-1574)

and "The History of Jacob," and many others, were lost forever. The French occupational government sent them to the Napoleonic Museum in Paris, but they never arrived. Napoleon himself stayed at the Palazzo Pitti multiple times, and in 1809, he housed his sister Elisa there, granting her the honorary title of Grand Duchess of Tuscany.

When the Napoleonic Wars ended and the French left Tuscany, the old order was restored, and the Habsburgs returned to the Palazzo Pitti. In 1833, Grand Duke Leopold II opened part of the palace to the public as an art museum. However, due to the Habsburgs' strong opposition to the unification of Italy in 1859-1861, all their Tuscan property was confiscated after the Grand Duchy was annexed to the Kingdom of Italy. Consequently, the Palazzo Pitti briefly became the residence of the first King of Italy, Victor Emmanuel II, as commemorated by Annibale Gatti's fresco, "The Genius of the House of Savoy" in the Palazzina della Meridiana in the Boboli Gardens. This is where the Costume Gallery—Italy's largest collection dedicated to the history of fashion—is now located.

Besides the Costume Gallery, the Palazzo Pitti complex houses the collections of the Palatine Gallery, the Gallery of Modern Art, the Silver Museum, the Porcelain Museum, and the Carriage Museum. Detailed information about exhibition schedules and booking tickets is available in the "Palazzo Pitti" section of the official Uffizi Gallery website.

In the Boboli Gardens, special attention should be paid to the "Buontalenti Grotto"—a masterpiece of Mannerist architecture created by Giorgio Vasari and Bernardo Buontalenti (primarily the latter, hence the name of the grotto) at the behest of Grand Duke Francesco I de' Medici. The unique decor of this pavilion imitates natural forms delicately interwoven with marvelous sculptural and pictorial compositions. On either side of the entrance stand the statues of Apollo and Ceres by Baccio Bandinelli. The central theme of this architectural marvel is the metamorphosis of chaos into order, the transformation of primordial matter into a finished creation—a core concept of alchemical philosophy, passionately pursued by Grand Duke Francesco I (as well as many other European rulers of the 16th and 17th centuries). The creator of all these stunning forms, corals, shells, and stalactites, from which anthropomorphic figures seem to crystallize, was the plaster master Pietro Mati.

6

Practical advice:

Where to stay in Florence

In this section, you will find a selection of excellent Florence hotels, inns, and hostels, some of which will not only provide you with comfortable accommodations in the city of Dante and Michelangelo but also help you momentarily lose track of time (a sensation that is your best ally when you are traveling through Tuscany).

Hostels

Ostello Gallo d'Oro

- Cozy and clean hostel with a good location.
- Address: Via Camillo Cavour, 104, 50129 Firenze FI
- +39 055 552 2964
- info@ostellogallodoro.com
- Features: Free Wi-Fi, breakfast included, shared and private rooms.

This is a very clean and cozy hostel that offers guests a delicious and varied breakfast. The staff is extremely pleasant and always available to answer questions about the city (if you have any left after reading this guide, of course). The hostel is within walking distance of the city center and all major attractions. However, the bustling Camillo Cavour Street and the shared bathrooms, which might have queues in the evening, can be a bit inconvenient. Overall, this hostel offers an excellent balance of price and quality.

Plus Florence

- Modern hostel with a variety of amenities, including a pool and fitness center.
- Address: Via Santa Caterina d'Alessandria, 15, 50129 Firenze FI
- +39 055 628 6347
- Features: Swimming pool, bar, terrace, common and private rooms.

Conveniently located, this hotel offers a wide range of included and additional services, as well as a pool, a fitness center, and a rooftop bar with a beautiful view of the city. The rooms are spacious and clean, though the relatively weak Wi-Fi signal and potential street noise at night are worthy of note.

Hostel Archi Rossi

- Popular hostel with good reviews and a cozy atmosphere.
- Address: Via Faenza, 94R, 50123 Firenze FI
- +39 055 290804
- Features: Breakfast included, garden, city tours, shared and private rooms.

This hostel is located just a few minutes' walk from Florence's train station, near the old city center. It offers top-notch service, and the rooms are simple yet comfortable. Breakfast is varied and included in the price of the stay. Additionally, the hostel provides an extra service of organized evening tours of the city for guests.

Inexpensive hotels

Hotel Dali

- Cozy and affordable hotel in the city center.
- Address: Via dell'Oriuolo, 17, 50122 Firenze FI
- +39 339 576 9086
- Features: Free Wi-Fi, close to major attractions.

The hotel is conveniently located within walking distance of Piazza del Duomo. The rooms are always clean and furnished quite cozily. However, please keep in mind that there are no elevators.

Hotel Alessandra

- Family-run hotel with a friendly atmosphere and good services.
- Address: Borgo Santi Apostoli, 17, 50123 Firenze FI
- +39 055 283 438
- Features: Breakfast included, free Wi-Fi, convenient location.

Conveniently located in the heart of Florence, just a few minutes' walk from Piazza della Signoria, this hotel offers clean, cozy, and spacious rooms. The breakfast is varied and tasty (though the selection could be larger).

Some inconveniences might include the old and slow elevator and the potential of noise from the street due to the hotel's location in the tourist center.

Hotel Casci Florence

- Small family-run hotel with excellent service.
- Address: Via Camillo Cavour, 13, 50129 Firenze FI
- +39 055 211686
- Features: Breakfast included, free Wi-Fi.

This hotel is situated in the historic center of Florence, just a few minutes from Piazza del Duomo. It offers comfortable rooms, breakfast included in the price, and friendly staff (as is the case with the other hotels I recommend). This hotel provides excellent value for the money and great service. Minor drawbacks include street noise and a somewhat repetitive breakfast.

Mid-range hotels

Hotel Loggiato dei Serviti

- A hotel with historical charm and comfortable rooms.
- Address: Piazza della Santissima Annunziata, 3, 50122 Firenze FI
- +39 055 289592
- Features: Breakfast included, free Wi-Fi, historic building.

This hotel is located right on Piazza Santissima Annunziata, near the Accademia Gallery. It stands out for its antique interiors, crafted with great attention to detail. They instantly set the timeless tone for your journey through Florence. Guests will also appreciate the varied and delicious breakfast included in the room rate.

Minor drawbacks include small windows in some rooms and an old elevator, which, though perfectly fitting the hotel's overall style, might be inconvenient for some guests.

Hotel Davanzati

- Comfortable and modern hotel.
- Address: Via Porta Rossa, 5, 50123 Firenze FI
- +39 055 286666
- Features: Free Wi-Fi, breakfast included, bar.

Located in the heart of Florence, this hotel allows you to reach all the city's main attractions within minutes on foot. The rooms are clean, cozy, and comfortable, though they might seem a bit small.

The central location can result in nighttime noise, which might prevent a peaceful night's sleep.

Hotel Santa Maria Novella

- A cozy hotel with a beautiful interior and convenient location.
- Address: Piazza di Santa Maria Novella, 1, 50123 Firenze FI
- +39 055 271840
- Features: Breakfast included, free Wi-Fi, fitness center.

The interiors of this hotel will set the tone for your trip from the very first moments of your stay. The spacious and elegant rooms, furnished in an eclectic classical style, offer stunning views that, combined with first-class service, will leave you impressed. Also worth noting is the varied breakfast included in your stay.

Hotel Torre Guelfa Palazzo Acciaiuoli

- A hotel with historical charm, located in the center of Florence.
- Address: Borgo Santi Apostoli, 8, 50123 Firenze FI
- +390552396338
- Features: Historical building, central location, great views, rooftop terrace.

Palazzo Acciaiuoli, named after its most famous owner—the Grand Seneschal of the Kingdom of Naples, patron of the arts, and friend and correspondent of Boccaccio and Petrarch, Niccolò Acciaiuoli, Count of Melfi, Malta, Gozo, and Baron of Corinth—was constructed in the 13th century. The building's commissioners and initial owners were members of another noble Florentine family, the Buondelmonti. It is believed that the feud between the Buondelmonti and Amidei families marked the beginning of the bloody rivalry between the Florentine Guelphs and Ghibellines (with the Buondelmonti aligned with the Guelphs and the Amidei with the Ghibellines; hence, the tower adjoining the palazzo is called Torre Guelfa). The

Buondelmonti family initially resided here on Borgo Santi Apostoli, and their 13th-century tower, which later became part of the 15th-century family palazzo, still stands on the nearby Via delle Terme. In 1341, the palazzo was purchased by Niccolò Acciaiuoli, son of the prominent Florentine banker and politician Acciaiolo Acciaiuoli (d. 1349) and Guglielmina de' Pazzi, cousin of the infamous Jacopo Pazzi. Leveraging his father's connections, Niccolò built a distinguished career at the court of King Robert of Anjou, who bestowed upon him the title of Grand Seneschal (effectively, the supreme commander of the army and the highest judge of the kingdom). Niccolò Acciaiuoli is said to have become the lover of King Robert's daughter-in-law, Catherine de Valois, for whom he secured the Principality of Achaea (on the Peloponnese peninsula). Catherine de Valois had legitimate claims to this principality, but it had long been usurped by another family. For these services, Acciaiuoli was awarded the title of Baron of Corinth (an ancient city on the Peloponnese that became a crucial fortress and trade center in the Principality of Achaea during the Crusader period). In his later years, Niccolò Acciaiuoli, one of the wealthiest nobles of Naples and Florence, funded the construction of the Certosa di Firenze, a Carthusian monastery completed after his death in 1365. He and many of his family members were interred there. The monastery is located five kilometers south of the old center of Florence. Although it is not included in my general city tour, I highly recommend visiting it if you have the time.

Niccolò Acciaiuoli's memory is preserved on the façade of the Cathedral of Santa Maria del Fiore and by the prominent Florentine artist Andrea del Castagno in his series of frescoes at Villa Carducci-Pandolfini (the originals of which are now in the Uffizi Gallery), where Acciaiuoli is depicted alongside Dante, Boccaccio, and Petrarch. Additionally, above the entrance to the palazzo, you can see the combined coat of arms of the Acciaiuoli and Buondelmonti families: two lions holding banners with the heraldic lilies of the House of Anjou (these banners were added to the Acciaiuoli arms by King Robert in recognition of Niccolò's faithful service to his house) and a cross on top of Golgotha, referring to the meaning of the family names, including Buondelmonti ("Good from the Mountain").

Niccolò Acciaiuoli also bequeathed the palace to the Carthusian monastery, which owned it until the 19th century, when secularization of monastic properties in Tuscany took place. The Palazzo Acciaiuoli was subsequently sold several times and eventually came into the possession of the Burresi Pettini family, who converted part of it into a superb hotel offering a unique blend of historical charm and modern comfort in the heart of Florence. I can assure you that your journey to the capital of the Italian Renaissance will be truly unforgettable if, after exploring the Uffizi Gallery and Piazza del Duomo, you return to your room within one of the oldest Florentine palaces—a place deeply connected to the history of an influential patrician family.

However, the hotel does have a few drawbacks. The historic building lacks an elevator, which might create an inconvenience for guests with heavy luggage or mobility issues. Additionally, due to the hotel's central location and insufficient soundproofing, some rooms might experience noise.

High-end hotels

Four Seasons Hotel Firenze

- A luxury hotel with excellent service and extensive gardens.
- Address: Borgo Pinti, 99, 50121 Firenze FI
- +39 055 26261
- Features: Spa, swimming pool, restaurants, gardens, free Wi-Fi.

The Four Seasons Hotel Firenze impresses guests with its luxurious service and magnificent location. The hotel offers spacious, elegantly decorated rooms with stunning views of the private garden, which is open to guests. The hotel staff stands out for their attention to detail and friendly approach, making the stay even more comfortable. The breakfast features a variety of delicious dishes.

Hotel Savoy

- An elegant hotel in the heart of Florence, with stunning views.
- Address: Piazza della Repubblica, 7, 50123 Firenze FI
- Features: Restaurant, fitness center, free Wi-Fi, bar.

The name of this hotel speaks for itself. You will enjoy spacious and elegant rooms, first-class service, and a friendly staff, along with a varied and delicious breakfast. Its perfect location in the heart of Florence offers excellent views from the rooms.

7

Where to eat in Florence

It is important to note that in Tuscany, you will encounter three main types of establishments:

- " Trattoria" : Often simple, family-run taverns in classic Tuscan style, with affordable prices and a pleasant atmosphere.

- " Osteria" : Originally humble drinking establishments or inns, now often wine bars with a focus on fine dining.

- " Ristorante" : High-end Italian restaurants offering gourmet cuisine.

Additionally, Italian fast food is categorized as "tavola calda" ("hot table") and features tasty and inexpensive dishes, usually served for takeaway.

Street food and inexpensive cafes

1. Trattoria ZaZa

Address: Piazza del Mercato Centrale, 26R, 50136 Florence FI, Italy

Located near the central market, Trattoria ZaZa offers traditional Florentine dishes at reasonable prices. The menu features items such as ribollita (Florentine soup) and the renowned Florentine steak. The interior is simple yet cozy, adding an authentic charm to the place.

131

Prices: Main courses range from €10-20.

2. Osteria Santo Spirito

Address: Piazza Santo Spirito, 9R, 50125 Florence FI, Italy

This osteria is located on Piazza Santo Spirito, a bit farther from the center but well worth the walk. It serves traditional Tuscan dishes, such as truffle pasta and roasted vegetables. The warm and friendly atmosphere makes it an ideal spot for a relaxing lunch or dinner.

Prices: Main courses are around €12-18.

3. Trattoria Mario

Address: Via della Spada, 27R, 50123 Florence FI, Italy

Trattoria Mario is a small but popular establishment known for its homemade dishes and delicious cuisine. It offers traditional Florentine fare, such as tortelli and stewed meats.

Prices: Main courses range from €10-15.

All three of the aforementioned establishments are within walking distance from the Ostello Gallo d'Oro, the first on our list, and offer excellent options for a tasty and affordable lunch or dinner while maintaining an authentic Florentine dining experience.

4. Trattoria da Giorgio

Address: Via San Gallo, 30R, 50129 Firenze FI, Italy

This cozy trattoria offers traditional Tuscan cuisine at affordable prices. The menu features dishes such as Florentine steak and homemade pizza. The atmosphere is friendly and laid-back, making this restaurant an excellent choice for lunch or dinner.

Prices: Main dishes range from €10-15.

5. Osteria Vecchio Cancello

Address: Via dei Servi, 52R, 50122 Firenze FI, Italy

Located within walking distance of Plus Florence, Osteria Vecchio Cancello offers authentic Florentine cuisine in a traditional style. Signature dishes include ribollita (Florentine soup) and pizza cooked in a wood-fired oven. The interior is simple but cozy.

Prices: Main dishes range from €12-18.

6. La Burrasca

Address: Via del Leone, 50R, 50124 Firenze FI, Italy

This osteria, located a bit farther from Plus Florence but still within walking distance, offers homemade Tuscan dishes. The menu features simple yet delicious options like homemade pasta and braised meat. The establishment has a pleasant and relaxed atmosphere, making it an excellent choice for a leisurely lunch or dinner.

Prices: Main dishes range from €10-15.

These establishments provide a great selection of authentic and affordable dishes near the Plus Florence hostel, the second on my list, allowing you to enjoy genuine Florentine cuisine without significant expense.

7. Osteria Vini e Vecchi Sapori

Address: Via dei Magazzini, 3R, 50122 Firenze FI, Italy

Located in the heart of the city, Osteria Vini e Vecchi Sapori offers homemade Tuscan cuisine. Here, you can enjoy dishes such as ribollita (Florentine soup) and homemade pasta. The establishment boasts a cozy and traditional atmosphere, making it an excellent choice for an authentic lunch or dinner.

Prices: Main dishes range from €12-18.

8. Trattoria da Giorgio

Address: Via San Gallo, 30R, 50129 Firenze FI, Italy

This cozy trattoria, located near Hostel Archi Rossi, offers traditional Tuscan cuisine at reasonable prices. The menu features classic Florentine dishes, and the establishment itself is charmingly simple and cozy.

Prices: Main dishes range from €10-15.

These establishments are within walking distance of Hostel Archi Rossi, the third on my list, and provide excellent value for money while maintaining an authentic Florentine atmosphere.

9. Trattoria il Contadino

Address: Via dei Conti, 17R, 50123 Firenze FI, Italy

This traditional Florentine trattoria is just a few minutes' walk from Hotel Dali. It offers a varied menu of homemade Tuscan dishes, including ribollita, Florentine steak, and pasta. The simplicity and coziness of the interior create an authentic atmosphere.

Prices: Main dishes range from €10-15.

Mid-range restaurants

1. Buca Lapi

Address: Via del Trebbio, 1R, 50123 Firenze FI, Italy

This historic establishment is renowned for its traditional Florentine dishes and excellent wine list. Here, you can enjoy specialties like Florentine steak and pasta, as well as a selection of Tuscan wines.

Prices: Main dishes range from €20-30.

Feature: An outstanding wine list with a focus on local wineries.

2. La Giostra

Address: Borgo Pinti, 10R, 50121 Firenze FI, Italy

La Giostra is a 15-minute walk from Hotel Casci and is renowned for its authentic Tuscan dishes and friendly service. The restaurant offers a wide selection of wines, including excellent local and regional options. The cozy and atmospheric interior makes it an ideal place for a relaxing dinner.

Prices: Main dishes range from €20-30.

Feature: A diverse wine list with a focus on Tuscan and Italian wines.

3. Ristorante Romantico il Paiolo

Address: Via dei Neri, 8R, 50122 Firenze FI, Italy

Ristorante Romantico il Paiolo offers traditional Tuscan and Italian cuisine in a cozy and romantic setting. Located in the historic center of Florence, it is conveniently situated for dining during city strolls. The menu features a variety of dishes, including pasta, risotto, and meat delicacies. Desserts include traditional Tuscan sweets, among other options. The restaurant also boasts a fine selection of local wines, allowing for perfect pairings, with knowledgeable staff to assist with recommendations.

The restaurant's warm and romantic atmosphere makes it an ideal spot for a romantic dinner or a special celebration. The traditional Italian decor creates a welcoming ambiance.

Main dishes range from €20-30.

Appetizers and desserts range from €10-15.

4. La Nicchietta in Calimaruzza

Address: Via Calimaruzza, 1R, 50122 Firenze FI, Italy

La Nicchietta offers traditional Tuscan dishes in a cozy and authentic atmosphere. Located in a picturesque area of Florence, it is close to attractions such as Piazza della Signoria and the Duomo. The restaurant is renowned for its attention to detail and quality of food, allowing guests to enjoy genuine Florentine cuisine. The menu features a variety of traditional pasta, such as pasta with Bolognese sauce and pasta with truffles, meat dishes including the famous Florentine steak (bistecca alla fiorentina), and various risottos with seasonal ingredients. Desserts include traditional Italian options like tiramisu and panna cotta. A wide selection of Tuscan and Italian wines is also available.

Main dishes typically range from €15-25.

Appetizers and desserts are around €10-15.

5. Trattoria Lo Stracotto

Address: Via dell'Acqua, 2R, 50122 Firenze FI

This establishment is located in the historic center of Florence, making it convenient for those who want to enjoy delicious local cuisine after exploring the city. The restaurant is renowned for its dishes prepared according to traditional recipes and its attention to ingredient quality. The menu offers a variety of pasta dishes, including popular Tuscan recipes, and meat dishes such as steak and stews. A highlight is the stracotto, a specialty slow-cooked meat dish. Additionally, there is a wide selection of risottos, desserts, and local Tuscan wines.

Main courses range from €15-25.

Appetizers and desserts are typically around €10-15.

6. Locanda de' Medici

Address: Via della Stufa, 1, 50123 Firenze FI

This restaurant is located in the center of Florence and offers the opportunity to enjoy both traditional Italian dishes and local Tuscan specialties. It is known for its attention to the quality of ingredients and its excellent service. Locanda de' Medici features a cozy and traditional interior that offers a pleasant atmosphere for lunch or dinner. The decor includes elements of Italian classic design, adding to the overall charm of the establishment.

Main courses typically cost between €20-30.

Appetizers and desserts are around €10-15.

7. Trattoria Anita

Address: Via Faenza, 90, 50123 Firenze FI

Trattoria Anita is located in the historic center of Florence and is a popular choice among locals and tourists for its authentic Florentine cuisine and pleasant atmosphere. The restaurant offers a wide selection of traditional Italian dishes prepared with fresh, local ingredients. The interior maintains a cozy and relaxed ambiance, featuring traditional Italian decor. It's an ideal setting for lunch or dinner.

Main courses typically cost between €15-25.

Appetizers and desserts are around €10-15.

High-end restaurants

1. Osteria Vini e Vecchi Sapori

Address: Via dei Velluti, 1R, 50125 Firenze FI

This restaurant is located in the heart of Florence and is renowned for its traditional Tuscan dishes, which are prepared with high-quality ingredients. The menu features both classic Florentine dishes and modern interpretations of Tuscan cuisine. The restaurant also offers an exquisite wine list with an excellent selection of Tuscan and Italian wines.

Prices: Main courses range from €30-50.

Highlights: Polite and attentive service, cozy atmosphere.

2. Enoteca Pinchiorri

Address: Via Ghibellina, 87, 50122 Firenze FI

One of the most renowned restaurants in Florence, Enoteca Pinchiorri boasts three Michelin stars and offers a unique gastronomic experience. The restaurant specializes in modern Italian cuisine with a focus on authentic Tuscan ingredients. It is also famous for its impressive wine collection.

Prices: Main courses range from €70-150.

Highlights: Elegant interior, top-notch service, outstanding wine selection.

3. Borgo San Jacopo

Address: Borgo San Jacopo, 14, 50125 Firenze FI

Borgo San Jacopo, located in the Lungarno Collection Hotel, offers modern interpretations of traditional Tuscan cuisine. The restaurant has been awarded a Michelin star and is known for its refined approach to cooking. The interior is stylish and contemporary, creating the perfect atmosphere for an exquisite dining experience.

Prices: Main courses range from €40-70.

Highlights: A remarkable blend of tradition and modernity, elegant setting, and attentive service.

8

Florence Museums

1. **Museo di Palazzo Vecchio**

- Piazza della Signoria
- Tel. Ticket Office + 39 055 2768325
- musei.civici@comune.fi.it
- ticketsmuseums.comune.fi.it

This palace is also the seat of the city council. Unfortunately, that means on certain special occasions when institutional ceremonies are scheduled, the museum might be totally or partially closed to the public. Before planning a visit, check the museum website for closure information.

The 'Traces of Florence' section of the museum, on the ground floor of Palazzo Vecchio, can be visited free of charge. The opening hours are the same as for the rest of the museum. For safety reasons, visitors with backpacks are asked to carry them by hand along the tour route.

Tower and Patrol Walk

Access is not permitted for children under six years of age and is not recommended for visitors with mobility difficulties, heart patients, asthmatics, and those who suffer from vertigo or claustrophobia. An adult must accompany children under 18. In case of rain, access to the Tower is suspended. The visit ends at the Patrol Walk.

Museum

Access for disabled visitors is via the side entrance in Via dei Gondi.

The two main floors of the museum are wheel-chair accessible, but architectural barriers prevent access to the mezzanine floor and some of the educational activity locations.

Cloakroom

Situated on the ground floor in the Cortile della Dogana, in the ticket office area.

Visitors must leave all umbrellas, backpacks, and large bags in the cloakroom. There is no fee to use the cloakroom.

Students must leave their backpacks in the cloakroom.

Wheelchairs and strollers may be borrowed free of charge.

Lift

The lift, which is situated on the ground floor in the Cortile della Dogana, is only for the use of visitors with reduced mobility.

2. Orsanmichele Church and Museum

- Via dell'Arte della Lana, 50123 Firenze FI
- Tel. Ticket Office + 055294883 .
- mn-bar.orsanmichele@cultura.gov.it
- bargellomusei.it

The museum does not have facilities for disabled access.

3. Chiesa di San Carlo dei Lombardi

- Via dei Calzaiuoli, 29, 50123 Firenze FI
- Tel./fax: +39 055 986 1648
- sancarlo-firenze.it

This is a working church. Admission is free but might be restricted due to Mass.

4. Giotto's Bell Tower

- Cathedral of Santa Maria del Fiore, Piazza del Duomo, 50122 Firenze FI

- +39 055 2645789
- help@duomo.firenze.it
- tickets.duomo.firenze.it

Accessibility

Before entering, visitors who climb the Bell Tower must leave the following inside the Luggage Storage (Piazza Duomo n. 38/r): suitcases, backpacks, parcels, containers, large and medium-sized bags, and other types of objects. (See the complete regulations at this link.) Visitors who present themselves at the entrance with prohibited objects will not be able to enter.

No lift is available, and there are many steps. The climb is not recommended for people with heart conditions or those suffering from dizziness or claustrophobia. Free admission can be reserved for people with mobility difficulties via email (accessibilita@duomo.firenze.it) or by contacting the cash desk in Piazza Duomo 14. This is subject to availability and the presentation of a certification document.

5. **Santa Maria del Fiore**

- Cathedral of Santa Maria del Fiore, Piazza del Duomo, 50122 Firenze FI
- +39 055 2645789
- help@duomo.firenze.it
- tickets.duomo.firenze.it

Accessibility

Admission to the cathedral is restricted to people wearing clothing suitable for a place of worship. Visitors with bare legs and shoulders or those who are wearing sandals, hats, or sunglasses will not be allowed inside the cathedral. Bulky backpacks and bags are also not allowed. The entrance for people with motor disabilities or impaired mobility is located on the right side of the cathedral.

Every first Thursday of the month at 3:00 pm, there are free guided tours for the blind and visually impaired; advance registration is required, and the number of participants is limited.
Reservations: +39 055 302885 and accessibilita@operaduomo.firenze.it

6. The Baptistery of Saint John

- Cathedral of Santa Maria del Fiore, Piazza del Duomo, 50122 Firenze FI
- +39 055 2645789
- help@duomo.firenze.it
- tickets.duomo.firenze.it

Visitors are advised that the Baptistery is undergoing restoration of the mosaics of the vault, so they are not visible.

Accessibility
The Baptistery is accessible to people with disabilities. It is possible to reserve free entry for a person with disabilities by writing to accessibilita@duomo.firenze.it or visiting the ticket office in Piazza Duomo 14. This is subject to availability and the presentation of a certification document.

7. Dome of Santa Maria del Fiore

- Cathedral of Santa Maria del Fiore, Piazza del Duomo, 50122 Firenze FI
- +39 055 2645789
- help@duomo.firenze.it
- tickets.duomo.firenze.it

Accessibility
Before entering, visitors who climb the dome must leave the following inside the Luggage Storage (Piazza Duomo n. 38/r):

suitcases, backpacks, parcels, containers, large and medium-sized bags, and other types of objects. (See the complete regulations at this link.) Visitors who present themselves at the entrance with prohibited objects will not be able to enter.

The dome can be accessed only by booking a slot time No lift is available, and there are many steps. The climb is not recommended for people with heart conditions or those suffering from dizziness or claustrophobia.

Free admission can be reserved for people with mobility difficulties via email at accessibilita@duomo.firenze.it or by contacting the cash desk in Piazza Duomo 14. This is subject to availability and the presentation of a certification document.

8. **The Duomo Terraces**

- Cathedral of Santa Maria del Fiore, Piazza del Duomo, 50122 Firenze FI
- +39 055 2645789
- help@duomo.firenze.it
- tickets.duomo.firenze.it

Accessibility
The terraces can be accessed only on a contingent basis with one of our companions or guides, following the rhythms of the slot and not independently. No lift is available, and there are many steps. The climb is not recommended for people with heart conditions or those suffering from dizziness or claustrophobia. Bulky backpacks and bags are not allowed. Free admission can be reserved for people with mobility difficulties via email at accessibilita@duomo.firenze.it or by contacting the cash desk in Piazza Duomo 14. This is subject to availability and the presentation of a certification document.

9. Ancient Basilica of Santa Reparata

- Cathedral of Santa Maria del Fiore, Piazza del Duomo, 50122 Firenze FI
- +39 055 2645789
- help@duomo.firenze.it
- tickets.duomo.firenze.it

Accessibility
Access is from the Cathedral "Porta Campanile" (south side, beside the Bell Tower entrance).
Visitors arrive at Santa Reparata by descending a short staircase in the second bay of the right aisle of the cathedral (no lifts).

10. Casa Martelli

- Via Ferdinando Zannetti, 8, 50123 Firenze FI
- +390550649420
- bargellomusei.it

Accessibility
The museum is equipped with facilities for disabled access. The use of scooters and electric wheelchairs is limited and assessed on a case-by-case basis to ensure the safety of museum spaces and artworks.

11. Cappelle Medicee

- Piazza di Madonna degli Aldobrandini, 6, 50123 Firenze FI
- +390550649430
- bargellomusei.it
- Closed: Tuesdays, Christmas holidays

Accessibility

The museum is equipped with facilities for disabled access. The sidewalk is seamlessly connected to the street. Wheelchair accessibility on the ground floor is made possible through a ramp. The use of scooters and electric wheelchairs is limited and assessed on a case-by-case basis to ensure the safety of museum spaces and artworks.

To reach the Cappella dei Principi on the first floor, an elevator is available. From there, access to the Sagrestia Nuova is provided through a platform lift. Restrooms and the bookshop are accessible along the exit route.

"Michelangelo's Secret Room"

Visits are available by reservation only. For more information, visit the Tickets section.

Each visit lasts 15 minutes, with a maximum of four people per time slot.

Access and exit are via a narrow staircase with 12 steps. Unfortunately, no elevator is available, and the room is not accessible to individuals with disabilities or mobility limitations. Additionally, entrance to children under 10 years old and unaccompanied minors is not allowed.

Access is not recommended for individuals with heart conditions or claustrophobia or for women in advanced stages of pregnancy.

Prior to entry, please deposit luggage, backpacks, large and medium-sized packages, umbrellas, and any other large items deemed unsuitable by our security staff on the upper floor.

Cloakroom

Small bags or backpacks are allowed in the museum. Key lockers are available; they are activated with a deposit of 1€, which is returned when the locker is reopened.

Due to the limited number of lockers available, student groups cannot use them. Large luggage, suitcases, and oversized backpacks are not allowed. Umbrellas must be carried with you during your visit.

12. Palazzo Medici Riccardi

- Via Camillo Cavour, 3, 50129 Firenze FI
- +390552760552
- palazzomediciriccardi.it
- info@palazzomediciriccardi.it
- Closed: Wednesdays and December 25

Tickets to Palazzo Medici Riccardi include admission to the Palace, with the Cappella dei Magi (Chapel of the Magi) and Galleria degli Specchi (Mirror Gallery), as well as access to the Archaeological Itinerary, Marble Museum, and ongoing temporary exhibitions.
The number of visitors allowed inside the Chapel of the Magi at any one time is restricted to allow access to all those visiting the premises. Access is limited to 10 people every five minutes, and the visit duration is five minutes. You might be asked to wait in the Coloumn Courtyard before entering.

Accessibility
All the exhibition rooms of Palazzo Medici Riccardi, except the Chapel of the Magi, are fully accessible to people with impaired mobility. The Chapel of the Magi is accessible (by means of a special platform) to wheelchairs that measure a maximum of 70 cm in width and whose total weight is not greater than 250 kg.
Upon request, a wheelchair is available at the info point.
Access for visitors with impaired mobility is from Via Ginori no.2.

13. Accademia Gallery of Florence

- Via Ricasoli, 58/60, 50129 Firenze FI
- +390550987100
- galleriaaccademiafirenze.it
- Closed: Mondays, January 1, December 25

Useful Information

To access the museum and ensure everyone's safety, visitors must go through a security inspection.

Items like scissors, blades, and any other metal object that could pose a danger to people or the artworks on display will be collected by the security staff at the entrance to the museum and left at the metal detector.

The museum does not have a cloakroom. Therefore, visitors with large bags and backpacks, helmets, etc., will not be allowed to enter. Visitors can bring bottles of water that do not exceed half a liter.

Lost items

Objects left at the metal detector and not collected on the day of the visit will remain in custody at the museum until the first Tuesday of the following month. After this date, they will be considered lost objects and delivered, in accordance with current legislation, to the Lost and Found Office of the Municipality of Florence.

The same procedure will be followed for objects lost by visitors inside the museum. The museum does not under any circumstances provide for the shipment of forgotten or lost objects.

Accessibility

The museum is equipped with facilities for persons with disabilities. The entrance and ticket office are accessible from Via Ricasoli 60. Each of the halls and galleries that are open for exhibition is completely wheelchair accessible.

Lift

The museum is equipped with a lift to reach the upper floor.

14. Medici Museum

- Piazza Filippo Brunelleschi, via degli Alfani, Via del Castellaccio, 50121 Firenze FI
- museodemedici.org
- museodemedici@gmail.com

15. **Innocenti Museum**

- Piazza della Santissima Annunziata, 13 50122 Florence
- +39 055 203 7122
- museodeglinnocenti.it

Accessibility
For people with disabilities or reduced mobility, the Museo degli Innocenti is accessible from the main entrance. Lifts can be used to reach various floors.
The entire museum can be visited.
Toilets for people with disabilities are located along the tour route.
The Museo degli Innocenti and its " artworks to be touched"
This project that aims to make some of the artworks of the Innocenti museum accessible to visually impaired and blind users.
Along the museum itinerary—from the history section, through the courtyards, to the art section—a series of 10 original works of art is accessible to visually impaired and blind visitors. Simply wear special latex gloves to discover The Coat of Arms of the Silk Art, the marble font in the Courtyard of Men, the Coronation of the Virgin by Benedetto Buglioni, and many other works!

16. **National Archaeological Museum of Florence**

- P.za della SS. Annunziata, 9b, 50121 Firenze FI
- +3905523575
- cultura.gov.it

Please note! From July 2024 to the end of December 2025, the museum will be partially closed for reconstruction. Inconveniences during visits are possible.

17. **Leonardo da Vinci Interactive Museum**

- Via dei Servi, 66/R, 50122 Firenze FI
- +39055282966
- leonardointeractivemuseum.com

In honor of the museum's 20th anniversary, a 50% discount is available on tickets purchased online. In addition, with an online ticket, you are guaranteed entry at the specified time, even if there is a line.

18. **INPS Toscana—Palazzo Pazzi**

- Via del Proconsolo, 10, 50122 Firenze FI
- +3905343011343

A creative and art space for various exhibitions, this is part of the EXIBART network.

19. **Museo Nazionale del Bargello**

- Via del Proconsolo, 4, 50122 Firenze FI
- +390550649440
- bargellomusei.it

Accessibility

The museum is equipped with facilities for disabled access. The pavement is seamlessly connected to the street level. The use of scooters and electric wheelchairs is limited and evaluated on a case-by-case basis to ensure the safety of museum spaces and artworks. The museum's rooms (except for the chapel and the sacristy) are accessible; any elevation differences can be overcome with ramps (staff assistance is available) and an elevator. Some thresholds have slight elevation. Access to the Michelangelo Hall is through the bookshop; the exit is through the same. Adequate restroom facilities are available on the second floor.

Paths for visually impaired and blind visitors

Visually impaired visitors interested in exploring the Museo Nazionale del Bargello can contact Educational Services to receive guidance on the planned route within the museum, with the possibility of arranging a specific date for their visit:

Tel. +39 055 0649444 (Tuesday and Wednesday from 9:00 am to 12:00 pm)

Email: mn-bar.didattica@cultura.gov.it

To touch selected sculptures, a pair of gloves, available at the museum's ticket office, is required. Additionally, a tactile path diagram for non-sighted and visually impaired visitors is available for consultation at the ticket office.

Cloakroom

The cloakroom is located in front of the ticket office. There, visitors must leave umbrellas, large backpacks, and bulky bags. Oversized luggage, suitcases, and excessively large backpacks are not allowed. The service is complimentary.

20. **Basilica of the Holy Cross**

- Piazza di Santa Croce, 16, 50122 Firenze FI
- +390552008789
- santacroceopera.it
- ticket.santacroceopera.it

Accessibility

Visitors with impaired movement or those in wheelchairs can access the basilica and the cloister via a ramp and raised platform. The ramp is situated on the north side of the basilica in Largo Bargellini, while the platform is situated at the cloister exit onto Piazza Santa Croce. Please note that admission for visitors with disabilities and their caregivers is free of charge and enjoys priority, with no need to book.

Guide-dogs used by visitors with impaired sight or hearing and holding the appropriate certification are welcome.

21. **Pazzi Chapel**

- Largo Piero Bargellini, 50122 Firenze FI
- +390552466105

Pazzi Chapel is part of the Basilica of the Holy Cross complex and can be visited with a single ticket.

22. **Church of San Remigio**

- Piazza S. Remigio, 50122 Firenze FI
- +39055284789

This is an active Catholic church and might not always be available for visiting.

23. **Palazzo Gondi**

- Via dei Gondi, 2, 50122 Firenze FI
- +390552670177
- gondi.com

This is private property. To inquire about viewing the interior, please complete the feedback form on the family website.

24. **The Uffizi Gallery**

- Piazzale degli Uffizi, 6, 50122 Firenze FI
- +39055294883
- ffizi.it/gli-uffizi

Planning your visit

Prior to your visit, particularly during extremely busy times and in the case of single visitors, you should book your ticket online to avoid lengthy queues on admission. Booking is optional and incurs a fee, but it also reduces your wait time. The ticket allows for a single entry and cannot be reused. The museum staff might ask you to show your ticket at any point, so you should keep it accessible throughout the duration of your visit.

Backpacks, bags, umbrellas and other large objects must be stored in the cloakroom prior to entry. Storage is free. Visitors are subject to metal detector inspection in some museums.

At the Uffizi, a route for the visually impaired offers the opportunity to touch original sculptures from the Medici collection.

"Uffizi by touch" is a tactile journey that includes 15 original sculptures from the Medici family's archaeology collection.

It is designed to be enjoyed independently through a tactile orientation map provided free of charge at the ticket office along with a pair of gloves to be worn during the experience. The gloves are disposable and made of hypoallergenic material.

Each work is accompanied by captions in Braille and with enlarged characters for the visually impaired. These are available in both Italian and English.

The sculptures on the list are located along the corridors of the Gallery on the second floor and in the Niobe Hall and were selected for their archaeological interest and tactile qualities. They are protected by spacers that can be removed by contacting the security personnel.

Due to ongoing set-up work, the itinerary may be subject to change without prior notification.

For information about the works available for the tactile experience, please write, well in advance, to uffiziaccessibili@cultura.gov.it.

25. **Palazzo Pitti**

- Piazza de' Pitti, 1, 50125 Firenze FI
- +39055294883
- uffizi.it/palazzo-pitti

Accessibility

From the square, the climb to the entrance of the Pitti Palace is rather steep (with a maximum gradient of 20%), so an accompanying person is recommended for wheelchair users or persons with reduced mobility. The entire area is pedestrianized and cannot be accessed by vehicle. If you have a disabled person's badge, you can park nearby.

The ticket office is located to the right of the façade, on the same level as the entrance door, under an open loggia about 87 meters away.

There are no steps to enter the inner courtyard of the palace (the Cortile dell'Ammannati). The courtyard is the entrance space where some services are located (the cafeteria, bathroom, and bookshop), as well as the starting point for visiting the Pitti museums. From here, one can access the Boboli Gardens; on the left side of the courtyard is a vaulted corridor that leads to a road with a dirt and gravel track (uphill), which, in turn, leads to the amphitheater. The ordinary entrance, located in the courtyard near the cafeteria, involves climbing a winding incline (also known as a flat staircase) with 44 shallow steps and no handrail, which connects to a short paved slope leading to the amphitheater.

Treasury of the Grand Dukes Museum: located on the left side of the courtyard. The entrance door is also the exit of the museum; the threshold has a maximum height of 3 centimeters. The museum is set up on two floors connected by a staircase. This is why persons with reduced mobility can access only the ground floor.

From the courtyard, you can take the stairs or lifts to the Palatine Gallery (first floor) and the Gallery of Modern Art and the Museum of Costume and Fashion (second floor). The lifts are located on the right side of the courtyard, near the cloakroom.

The ordinary entrance involves climbing four flights of stairs (71 steps) to reach the Palatine Gallery. To reach the Gallery of Modern Art, you must climb another four flights of stairs (68 steps).

There are signs in the courtyard indicating the direction to reach the Pitti Palace museums and services.

9

City of troubles, harsh Pistoia…

Gabriele D'Annunzio, one of the most significant Italian poets of the 20th century, wrote about this city. It was founded as a Roman outpost during their conflict with the local Ligurian tribes and the conquest of their land in the 2nd century BCE. It was here, in 62 BCE, that the infamous Lucius Sergius Catiline perished in battle against the forces of the Roman Republic. Catiline, who attempted to seize power and establish his dictatorship, raised a rebellion and amassed an army of 20,000 men. According to legend, the body of the rebellious Catiline was buried in Pistoia itself (and not thrown into the river beheaded, as the ancient Roman historian Sallust wrote). That is why the oldest surviving medieval tower in the city, supposedly built over Catiline's grave in the 9th century, was named after him.

You can reach Pistoia from Florence either by train from Firenze Santa Maria Novella station or by car via the Via Toscana. In any case, the journey will not take long; this small town is very close to Florence, and the historic center of Pistoia is very close to the train station. Unlike Florence, whose winding medieval streets can be endlessly explored, Pistoia is a small town that can be fully experienced in just one day.

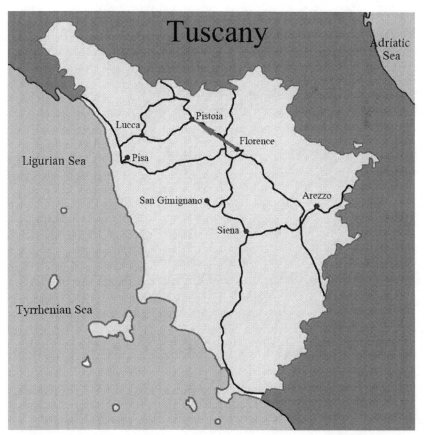

It is much more difficult to say anything about Pistoia as compared to Saturn-Florence, into whose orbit Pistoia has hopelessly fallen. Pistoia is now doomed to be just one of the many satellites of this giant until the end of the universe. Indeed, the spirit of Florence permeates every canvas, every stroke, every marble curve of Italian art, while Pistoia's fate has been less fortunate—sub umbra (in the shadow), occasionally drenched in blood.

As early as 1105, this town was a self-governing municipality, independent of any Italian feudal lord. For the next two centuries, it had its own government, consisting of elected consuls. During this time, Pistoia developed its own patrician class, particularly notable for the nine wealthiest and most influential families. Their rule is considered the city's golden age. However, as you might have guessed, the larger and more powerful neighbors of Pistoia—Lucca and, of course, Florence—could not ignore the prosperity of this independent city. In May 1305, Florentine and Lucchese troops arrived at the walls of Pistoia and began an 11-month siege that lasted until April 11, 1306. The new rulers of the city—the Florentines—immediately began to dominate the public life of Pistoia through their trusted representatives, drowning in blood any inhabitants who tried to rebel against Florence.

It is to this harsh period of the city's history, and partly to the fact that it was here where the rebellion of the ancient Roman politician Catiline met its tragic end, that the lines of Gabriele D'Annunzio, which I have used as the title of this section of the guide, are dedicated. The harsh truth we learn from all of human history is that the strong always oppress the weak. This has been the case, is the case, and will always be the case as long as humanity lives under the sun.

For Pistoia, this dismal state of affairs persisted until the beginning of the rule of Cosimo I de' Medici, who proclaimed himself Grand Duke of Tuscany in 1569. With his rise to power, a period of "restoration" of old municipalities began. This allowed Pistoia to regain its status as a cultural center. Academies and clubs for poetry, music, painting, and sculpture enthusiasts opened in the city. At the end of the 17th century, in the building of one of Pistoia's first academies (the Accademia dei Risvegliati), the city's first theater opened. It is known today as Teatro Manzoni and is located at Corso Gramsci 127. Although the theater's modern appearance is the result of a major reconstruction in the 1860s, it can rightly be considered the oldest theater in Pistoia.

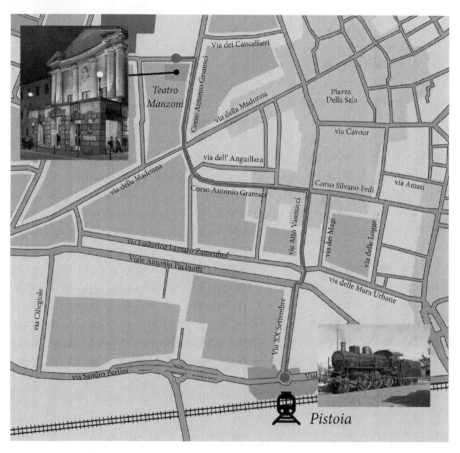

Piazza del Duomo and Cathedral of San Zeno

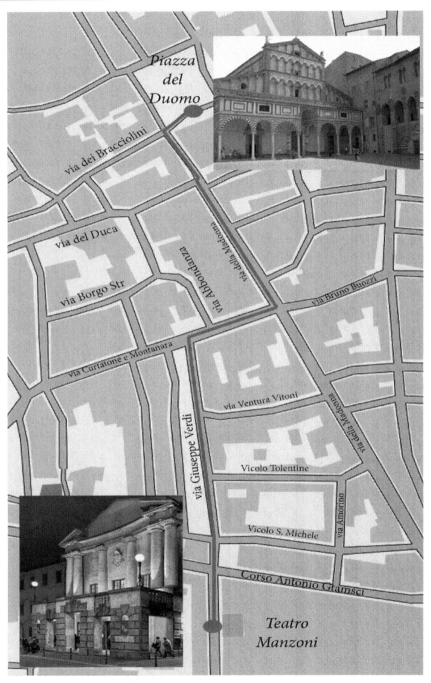

Here, in this small square, whose nearly complete square shape is defined by the surrounding buildings, all the main attractions of Pistoia are gathered as if on display—an attribute of many small Tuscan towns, which do not typically "spread their thoughts" along the banks of rivers but rather succinctly express their status in one concise statement. As in Florence, this square was formed at the intersection of the two main streets of any Roman city: the decumanus and the cardo, whose directions today correspond to Via degli Orafi and Via dei Bracciolini, respectively. Naturally, the main landmark of the square is the Cathedral of San Zeno, dedicated to Saint Zeno of Verona, who is venerated as the patron saint of Pistoia.

Of course, the church before you now did not emerge from nothing. As early as the 10th century AD, there was a church here, mentioned in ancient records but significantly damaged by fires in the 12th and 13th centuries. It was subsequently rebuilt and gradually altered, expanded, and adorned over the following centuries, as is the case with most ancient Italian churches. The current façade of the San Zeno Cathedral, which we see today, was constructed between 1379 and 1449. In the early 16th century, the renowned Florentine artist Andrea della Robbia worked on its decoration.

Perhaps, after Santa Maria del Fiore, the San Zeno Cathedral does not seem particularly impressive to you. (After all, what could seem so after the Florence Cathedral?) However, what attracted me most to the main church of Pistoia was not the façade but the interior, which serves as a fascinating metaphor: rather rough and sparsely decorated colonnades, separating the main nave from two side aisles, similarly gray and bare, converge in the central apse, richly decorated in the Mannerist style in the 17th century and adorned with frescoes by Domenico Cresti and the painting "Resurrection" by Cristofano Allori.

What might impress you the most in the San Zeno Cathedral is the silver altar of San Jacopo. It is located in the Chapel of the Crucifix. Over nearly two centuries, 12 masters worked on this masterpiece of silverwork, adorned with silver foil. Among them, Andrea di Jacopo d'Ognabene stands out as the author of the figures of the Apostles and saints in the upper central part of the altar and scenes from the New Testament in the lower central part. It is also likely that Filippo Brunelleschi himself contributed, with figures of saints and prophets attributed to him in the right part of the altar.

In addition, it is worth briefly mentioning the bell tower of the San Zeno Cathedral—rebuilt by Giovanni Pisano, incorporating part of the Lombard fortifications, and featuring an observation deck at its summit.

The building that almost adjoins the San Zeno Cathedral on the right side is none other than the Antico Palazzo dei Vescovi.

As if assembled from various parts of other buildings entirely different in form and style, this palazzo was constructed on the main square of Pistoia in the 11th century. It would be more accurate to say that the cathedral adjoins it rather than the other way around. Its intricate appearance combines elements of French Gothic and remnants of the Chapel of San Jacopo, where, incidentally, Dante's character Vanni Fucci, nicknamed "The Beast," committed his crime—the theft of church valuables—for which he was condemned to Hell in the "pit of thieves," where he was encountered by the most famous Florentine and his timeless companion, Virgil. The palazzo, gradually expanded and reconstructed over the centuries, developed its unique identity much like many of its contemporaries.

From the 15th century, the rooms on the ground floor of the palace were rented out to merchants, eventually making the bishop's residence resemble a series of shops. By the end of the 18th century, the Bishop of Pistoia, Scipione de' Ricci (whose name will appear again on this square), received permission from the Grand Duke of Tuscany, Pietro Leopoldo I, to build a new residence. The old palazzo was sold to private individuals. Divided into numerous shops, apartments, and stores, the palazzo lost its former appearance for a long time. Not until the early 20th century was the first restoration undertaken to transform the old Bishop's Palace into a museum, which opened in 1980.

Today, the museum associated with the San Zeno Cathedral houses, among other things, a stunning 16th-century Flemish tapestry once gifted to the Bishop of Pistoia and kept in the cathedral until 2016. This magnificent work of art, known as the "Millefiori Tapestry" or "Tapestry of a Thousand Flowers," measures 790x270 cm (25x8 feet) and depicts scenes of wildlife with various animals amidst a multitude of plants and flowers—hence its name.

Also part of the San Zeno Cathedral complex, the Baptistery of Saint John the Baptist, located opposite the cathedral's facade and also known as the Baptistery of San Giovanni in Corte, has an octagonal shape similar to that of the Florentine Baptistery, with which we are already familiar. Combining elements of Pisan, Florentine, and Sienese Gothic, this building is rightfully considered one of the masterpieces of the Tuscan direction of this architectural style. Standing about 40 meters tall, the baptistery is clad in white and green marble from Siena, Prato, and Carrara. Its interior is adorned with terracotta tiles, continuing the metaphorical contrast seen in the interior of the San Zeno Cathedral.

To the left of the San Zeno Cathedral, deeper into the square, stands a grey palazzo with five arches spanning three stories. This is the Palazzo degli Anziani, or Palazzo di Giano. It has housed the Pistoia City Hall for the past 700 years and, since 1922, has also hosted the civic city museum. The museum's collection, though not extensive, is highly intriguing, featuring works such as "Saint Francis, Stories of His Life and Miracles After Death," attributed to Coppo di Marcovaldo, and pieces by the Proto-Renaissance master Lippo di Benivieni.

To the left of this palazzo is an interesting 18th-century building—an unassuming three-story structure with the "Duomo" café on the ground floor. If you look closely, you will notice elements of marble decoration typical of Romanesque churches in Tuscany, similar to those on the facade of San Zeno Cathedral. An even closer inspection will reveal preserved apses, indicating that this building was once a church. Indeed, what you see before you is all that remains of the Santa Maria Cavaliera Church, which is likely several centuries older than the Pistoia Cathedral. The first mention of this church dates back to 979, and its name is connected to the knightly investiture ceremonies held there over time. However, in 1784, by decree of Bishop Scipione de' Ricci, the church was closed, and its building was sold to private individuals for the establishment of shops. This decision was part of the bishop's effort to reform his parish and reduce the influence of various monastic and knightly orders. Opposed to the popular Catholic cult of the Sacred Heart of Jesus, Scipione de' Ricci found himself in conflict with the Vatican. In 1790, after losing the support of Grand Duke Pietro Leopoldo I of Tuscany (who was elected Holy Roman Emperor that same year and left Tuscany), Scipione was forced to flee Pistoia to escape the ensuing unrest. In 1791, he officially resigned from his episcopal see.

Farther to the left of this three-story house is the famous Tower of Catiline, reputedly built on the burial site of the rebellious Roman general, as previously mentioned. This tower marks the culmination of Piazza del Duomo, the main square of Pistoia.

Basilica della Madonna dell'Umiltà (Shrine Basilica of Our Lady of Humility)

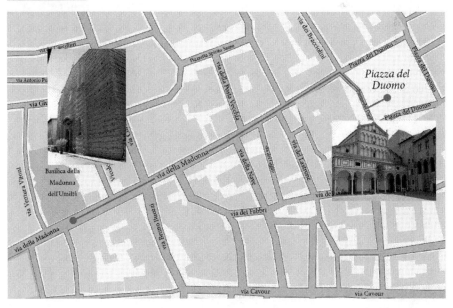

Following Piazza del Duomo along Via degli Orafi past the Palazzo del Podesta, also known as Palazzo Pretorio (constructed in 1367 to house the city government and still functioning as the city court), we soon reach Via della Madonna, which continues from Via degli Orafi after the intersection with Via Bruno Buozzi. Shortly, to our right, we will see another large church which, compared to the Cathedral of San Zeno and many other churches in Tuscany, might seem rough and almost devoid of elegance. In some sense, this architectural approach reinterprets the metaphor of the Pistoia Cathedral: You can't judge a book by its cover, especially when that book is the Holy Scripture.

For many decades, two of Pistoia's most noble families—the Panciatichi and the Cancellieri—were embroiled in a bloody feud. These noble lords spared no one: Women, children, and the elderly were hanged, beheaded, or burned alive in their homes alongside their husbands, fathers, and sons. The streets of Pistoia, dubbed "the city of sorrows" by Gabriele d'Annunzio, turned crimson whenever a Panciatichi or Cancellieri raised their heraldic banner. On one such bloody day, July 17, 1490, the parishioners of the Santa Maria Forisportae Church, located where the Basilica of Our Lady of Humility now stands, witnessed a true miracle: The image of the Virgin Mary on the chapel wall began to bleed. Indeed, a few drops of thick, crimson liquid appeared on the Virgin's forehead. Soon, half the city's residents gathered to witness the divine sign sent by the silent witness of so many terrible fratricides.

The mayor of the city, the people's captain, the gonfaloniere, city council members, and Bishop of Pistoia Nicollo Pandolfini arrived at the Santa Maria Forisportae chapel, officially confirming the miracle. Not long after, the heads of the Panciatichi and Cancellieri families— the indirect "culprits"—appeared in the chapel. Bishop Pandolfini interpreted the bloodstained sign as the Virgin's demand for peace between the city's two most influential families and their supporters. Reluctantly, Signor Cancellieri shook hands with Signor Panciatichi, and both solemnly vowed to eternalize their "humility before the will of the Lord" by erecting a worthy temple on the site of the old Santa Maria Forisportae Church. Thus, in 1495, local architect Ventura Vitoni began work on the future Basilica della Madonna dell'Umiltà based on a design by the more famous but likely recently disgraced Giuliano da Sangallo.

Vitoni devoted 27 years of his life to constructing the basilica but died in 1522 without completing it. After a period of stagnation, Grand Duke Cosimo I de' Medici entrusted the basilica's completion to his court sculptor and architect, the renowned "father of art history," Giorgio Vasari, whose main task was to crown the church with a worthy dome. In this regard, Vasari departed from Sangallo's original design, making the dome slightly larger and more massive. In its final form, Vasari's dome rises 59 meters (194 feet) above the stone streets of Pistoia. However, shortly after its completion in 1569, cracks appeared in the dome's structure. Vasari was forced to reinforce it in various ways. Yet, even this proved insufficient; perhaps Giorgio Vasari was simply not Filippo Brunelleschi. Over the following years, the dome underwent additional reinforcements and restorations, the latest of which occurred recently, at the beginning of this century.

Vasari never completed the basilica's facade, as he was consumed with the challenge of countering gravity with his enormous dome and thereby created that accidental dialogue with the Cathedral of San Zeno mentioned earlier. But did the basilica help reconcile Pistoia's two largest families? Alas, by 1537, members of the Cancellieri family, expelled from the city by their adversaries, sought refuge in the town of Cutigliano, just north of Pistoia. There, they were besieged by Panciatichi supporters. Trapped in the Church of Saint Bartholomew in Cutigliano, the Cancellieri decided to surrender to their enemies. However, as soon as they opened the church doors, an armed mob stormed in and slaughtered everyone inside before setting the church on fire. Thus, "stern Pistoia" claimed the Cancellieri for the last time.

Palazzo Cancellieri, the Ceppo Hospital, and the underground Pistoia

The story of the Cancellieri family did not end in the Church of Saint Bartholomew in Cutigliano. If you leave the Basilica of Our Lady of Humility and head along Via Curtatone e Montanara in the direction of traffic, you will soon see, on your left, a massive palazzo with abundant rustication on the corners. It will be at number 51. The Palazzo Ganucci Cancellieri was inherited by the family in an unfinished state at the end of the 16th century, when all past conflicts had subsided, and they were able to return to Pistoia in peace. Architect Jacopo Lafri worked on the exterior of this palace in the early 17th century, and in 1795, the last member of the Cancellieri family died within its walls. After this, the building was inherited by the Ganucci family. Today, the only reminder of its original owners is the large Cancellieri coat of arms adorning the main entrance. According to family legend, the founder of the lineage bore the nickname "The Boar," which the family emblem reflects.

Let us continue a bit farther and turn onto Via Abbi Pazienza, which, after crossing Via de' Rossi, becomes Via del Carmine and, after a slight turn, Via delle Pappe. Here, at the end of this street where it opens onto Piazza Papa Giovanni XXIII, your attention will inevitably be drawn to a building resembling Brunelleschi's "Ospedale degli Innocenti" in Florence—the Hospital del Ceppo. Its name translates directly as "Hospital of the Donation Box," and its founding likely dates back to 1277.

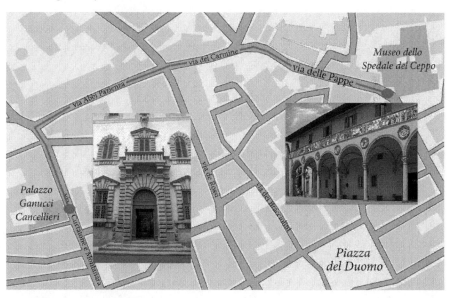

The building before us acquired its current appearance only in the 15th century, following the plague that struck Pistoia and other Tuscan cities. During this time, the Hospital del Ceppo became the city's main medical facility. Many residents who died from the plague bequeathed their movable and immovable property to the hospital. As a result, the "Company of Saint Mary," which managed the hospital, came into possession of numerous buildings and lands in Pistoia. This significant acquisition did not go unnoticed. In 1350, a year after the Black Death left Pistoia, city authorities decided to secularize the hospital, placing it under municipal management. This decision was reaffirmed in 1424, after Florence conquered Pistoia. It was then that the hospital began to expand.

As you might have guessed, the architects of the facade before you drew inspiration from Brunelleschi's "Ospedale degli Innocenti." In addition, the glazed terracotta decorations created in the early 16th century echo, albeit not exactly, the decorations of the renowned Florentine master's work. From that time on, based on the frieze by Andrea della Robbia, which depicts a scene resembling a medical lesson, the hospital del Ceppo began conducting lessons in medicine. However, the official opening of the "Medical School of Pistoia" took place in the hospital in 1666. In 1784, Grand Duke of Tuscany Pietro Leopoldo I confirmed its operation with his charter. The curriculum at this school was designed for three courses over two years each, and until 1844, it had departments of "Practical Medicine," "Surgical Institutions," "Anatomy," "Practical Affairs," and "Operations and Obstetrics." However, by the mid-19th century, due to low attendance, the school was closed, and from then until 2013, the hospital del Ceppo operated exclusively as a city hospital.

Today, this elegant building houses a medical museum featuring a collection of surgical instruments, ancient medical texts, an "apothecary laboratory," and an anatomical theater, which can also be visited during the "Underground Pistoia" tour organized by the Institute of Historical and Archaeological Research. This tour is a unique event, taking place along the longest underground route in Tuscany—900 meters (2952 feet). The tour route follows the ancient course of the Brana River, which once crossed the historic center of Pistoia but from the 12th century flowed through an artificial channel and by the 15th century had gone entirely underground. Since then, the Brana has invisibly connected the city's most important buildings:

hospitals (including the hospital del Ceppo), laundries, metallurgical plants, mills, and more. Today, the underground course of the Brana still holds the "ghosts" of Pistoia's old days: the vaults beneath the hospital del Ceppo, which once supported the dome of the catacombs when they were only partially filled with earth, the remains of ancient city walls, preserved building foundations eight centuries old, and much more. This route became accessible to all after extensive restoration, conservation, and disinfection of the catacombs, recently carried out by the company Publiacqua SPA. Tickets for one of the most unusual tours in Tuscany can be booked on the official Pistoia Sotterranea website.

10

Where to stay in Pistoia

Hostel

B&B Canto Alla Porta Vecchia

- Address: Via Curtatone e Montanara, 2, 51100 Pistoia
- Phone: +39 0573 27692
- Description: A small hostel with cozy rooms, offering breakfast and Wi-Fi. Located in the very heart of the city, it provides easy access to the main attractions.

The hostel is within walking distance of major landmarks. The staff is friendly and hospitable. The rooms are clean and cozy, with a well-thought-out interior. Guests are served a variety of homemade dishes and pies for breakfast.

Cons: The location can be noisy in the evenings. The Wi-Fi is slow, and the rooms and bathrooms might feel cramped. It is difficult to find parking nearby if you are traveling by car.

Inexpensive hotels

Casa Rowe B&B

- Address: Via Verdi, 1, 51100 Pistoia PT, Italy
- Phone: +39 389 604 4369
- Amenities: Coffee machine, free Wi-Fi

This is a small B&B located in the city center. It offers cozy and comfortable rooms with good design. The staff is friendly and welcoming. The hotel offers a classic Italian breakfast with coffee and pastries. There is no bar or restaurant on-site. The rooms might seem small, and street-facing rooms might experience some noise.

SMART Rooms Pistoia

- Address: Via della Stufa, 4, 51100 Pistoia PT, Italy
- Phone: +39 389 450 7833
- Amenities: Free Wi-Fi

This modern hotel offers stylish, comfortable, and minimalist rooms. The staff is attentive and friendly. The hotel serves a classic breakfast with coffee and pastries. Downsides include small rooms and insufficient soundproofing.

Mid-range hotels

Battistero Residenza d'Epoca

- Address: Piazza del Duomo, 12, 51100 Pistoia PT, Italy
- Phone: +39 0573 079220
- Amenities: Free Wi-Fi, Minibar, Coffee machine

This unique hotel is in the city center, located directly on Piazza del Duomo. The hotel is housed in a historic building, giving it a special charm. Notable for its elegant interiors, which retain original architectural elements, it offers high-level service and a personalized approach. The rooms are stylish and comfortable. The hotel serves breakfast with coffee, pastries, and fruits. Downsides include potential noise issues and the lack of an elevator.

Hotel Patria

- Address: Via Francesco Crispi, 8, 51100 Pistoia PT, Italy
- Phone: +39 0573 358800

- Amenities: Bar, free Wi-Fi, non-smoking rooms, facilities for disabled guests

Located within walking distance of major attractions, the hotel features clean and comfortable rooms. The staff is hospitable and friendly. The hotel offers a good breakfast. Downsides include potential internet issues, the need for room updates, and the lack of on-site parking.

11

Where to eat in Pistoia

Street food and inexpensive cafes

Pizzeria Partenope

- Address: Via Sigismondo Morelli Gualtierotti 13, 51100 Pistoia, Italy
- Phone: +39 0573 190 4742

Pizzeria Partenope offers delicious and authentic Neapolitan-style pizza. The menu features a variety of pizzas cooked in a wood-fired oven, including classics like margherita, pepperoni, Quattro Formaggi, and many more. The staff is friendly and attentive. The interior is styled traditionally, creating a cozy and relaxed atmosphere. Please note that there might be queues during peak hours.

Pizza prices range from €8-15.

La Tazza Rossa

- Address: Via Porta Carratica, 32, 51100 Pistoia, Italy
- Phone: +39 331 876 7268

La Tazza Rossa is a cozy and popular café-restaurant in Pistoia, offering a diverse menu and pleasant atmosphere. The establishment is highly rated for the quality of its food and beverages, with particular praise for its delicious coffee and desserts. The staff is often described as friendly and attentive, enhancing the overall dining experience. However, during peak hours, it can become crowded and noisy, which might slow down service. Overall, it is an excellent choice for those seeking a comfortable spot for breakfast, lunch, or dinner in the heart of Pistoia.

Prices for dishes are in the mid-range, varying from €5-20.

Caffè Valiani 1831

- Address: Via Camillo Benso Conte di Cavour 55, 51100 Pistoia, Italy
- Phone: +39 0573 178 1353

Caffè Valiani 1831 is one of the oldest cafés in Pistoia, having been in operation since 1831. The interior is designed in a historical style with elements of classic Italian decor, preserving the charm of an old establishment. The menu offers a variety of Italian dishes, snacks, sweets, and desserts, as well as a wide selection of coffee, tea, and other beverages. The staff is friendly and attentive.

Prices vary but typically range from €5-15.

Mid-range restaurants

Bisteccatoscana

- Address: Via Sant'Andrea, 30, 51100 Pistoia, Italy
- Phone: +39 328 438 2056

Bisteccatoscana is a Tuscan restaurant with a strong emphasis on meat dishes. The wine list features a selection of Tuscan varieties. The interior is cozy and elegant, decorated in a way that highlights the Tuscan style. The staff is attentive and professional.

Prices vary but generally fall within the medium to high range. The average check is approximately €25-50 per person.

Rosso Veneziano

- Address: Via Piero della Francesca 200, 51100 Pistoia, Italy
- Phone: +39 0573 33329

Rosso Veneziano is an intriguing establishment that might pique your interest in my next guidebook. This restaurant is renowned for its unique offerings of Venetian cuisine. The menu features a variety of Venetian dishes, such as risotto, seafood, polenta, and other specialties. Additionally, it offers a range of pasta, meat, and fish dishes. The interior is stylish and contemporary, with Venetian accents, creating a cozy and refined atmosphere. The staff is courteous and professional, with a good knowledge of the menu and helpful recommendations.

Prices are in the moderate range. The average check is approximately €20-40 per person, depending on your choice of dishes and drinks.

Il Giardino del Vinaino

- Address: Via di Stracceria 13, 51100 Pistoia, Italy
- Phone: +39 327 265 3651

Il Giardino del Vinaino is a traditional Tuscan restaurant that is popular among locals. The menu features classic Tuscan dishes such as pasta, meat dishes, antipasti, cheeses, and desserts. Local wines are also offered. The restaurant's interior is cozy and authentic, reflecting a traditional Tuscan atmosphere. The staff is polite and attentive, with a good knowledge of the menu and helpful recommendations for selecting dishes and wines.

Prices are in the moderate range. The average check is approximately €20-35 per person, depending on your choice of dishes and drinks.

High-end restaurants

Manzoni

- Address: Via Salvatore Quasimodo, 34, 51100 Pistoia, Italy
- Phone: +39 0573 28101

Manzoni is a restaurant with an elegant interior and a contemporary, creative take on Italian cuisine. The menu offers a range of modern Italian dishes, including pasta, meat and seafood dishes, as well as unique appetizers and desserts. A diverse selection of wines is also available. The staff is professional and attentive, with a solid understanding of the menu and good recommendations for dishes and wines. Reservations might be required.

Prices are in the mid to high range. The average check is approximately €30-60 per person, depending on your choice of dishes and drinks.

Incipit Ristorante

- Address: Via Francesco Crispi, 8, 51100 Pistoia, Italy
- Phone: +39 375 747 3062

Incipit Ristorante is an excellent choice for those seeking to enjoy modern Italian cuisine in a stylish and elegant setting. The restaurant offers a diverse menu with high-quality and innovative dishes, as well as a wide selection of wines and cocktails. The atmosphere is chic and suitable for various occasions: a romantic dinner, business meeting, or special event. The attentive and professional staff ensures a pleasant dining experience. However, there might be queues during peak hours.

Prices are in the mid to high range. The average check is around €30-60 per person, depending on your choice of dishes and drinks.

12

Museums of Pistoia

1. **Teatro Manzoni**

- Corso Antonio Gramsci, 129, 51100 Pistoia PT
- +390573991609
- teatridipistoia.it/teatro-manzoni

Hours
Tuesday, Thursday, and Friday, 4-7 pm
Wednesday, 11 am to 3 pm
Saturday, 10 am to 1 pm
(Monday closed)

2. **Cathedral of San Zeno**

- Piazza del Duomo, 51100 Pistoia PT
- +39057325095

This is an active Catholic church and might not always be available for visiting.

3. **Museum of the Antico Palazzo dei Vescovi**

- Piazza del Duomo, 7, 51100 Pistoia PT
- +39 0573 974267
- info@pistoiamusei.it

Hours

From April to October, Wednesday-Sunday, 10 am to 7 pm. From November to March, Wednesday-Sunday, 10 am to 6 pm.

4. Battistero di San Giovanni in Corte

- Piazza del Duomo, 51100 Pistoia PT
- +393341689419

Hours

From Thursday to Monday, 10 am to 1 pm and 3-6 pm. Closed on Tuesdays and Wednesdays.

5. Bell Tower of the Cathedral of San Zeno

- Piazza del Duomo, 51100 Pistoia PT

The bell tower of the Cathedral of San Zeno stands at 66 meters high. Climbing to the top to admire the view of the city is a " can't-miss" experience.

Hours

From Wednesday to Monday, 10 am to 1 pm and 3-6 pm. Closed on Tuesday.

Visit only with an accompanying person. Please note that the ascent consists of 200 steps. There is no elevator. The ascent is not recommended for visitors with mobility difficulties, heart patients, asthmatics, and those who suffer from vertigo or claustrophobia. Children under 18 must be accompanied by an adult.

6. Palazzo degli Anziani: Civic Museum of Ancient Art in the Town Hall

- Piazza del Duomo, 1, 51100 Pistoia PT
- +39 0573 371296

Accessibility
The museum is accessible.
Admission is free for the disabled person and their companion.

7. **Shrine Basilica of Our Lady of Humility**

- Via della Madonna, 51100 Pistoia PT
- +39057322045

Hours
Monday through Friday, 8:30 am to 6 pm. Saturday and Sunday, 8:30 am to 7 pm.

Entry
Free

8. **Palazzo Ganucci Cancellieri**

- Via Curtatone e Montanara, 51, 51100 Pistoia PT

9. **Museo dello Spedale del Ceppo**

- Piazza Papa Giovanni XXIII, 14, 51100 Pistoia PT
- +390573371023

Hours
Winter (September 30, 2023 / June 2, 2024)
Tuesday to Friday, 10 am to 2 pm
Saturday, Sunday, and holidays, 10 am to 6 pm
Christmas and New Year's Eve, 4-7 pm
Monday closed
Summer (June 4 / September 29, 2024)
Tuesday to Friday, 3-7 pm
Saturday, Sunday, and holidays (July 25 and August 15),

Friday July 26 and August 16, 11 am to 7 pm
Monday closed
The ticket office closes 30 minutes before closing.

10. **Pistoia Sotteranea (Pistoia Underground)**

- Piazza Papa Giovanni XXIII, 15, 51100 Pistoia PT
- +39 0573 368023
- irsapt.it/it/pistoia-sotterranea

Access is available to people with motor disabilities through access ramps and an experimental system of Braille panels with diagrams of the underground plan for the blind.

13

Mobility tips

Florence Amerigo Vespucci Airport

- Via del Termine, 11, 50127 Firenze FI
- +39 055 306-18-30

Florence's airport, named after the famous explorer Amerigo Vespucci, is located in the Peretola district northwest of the city center.

Taxi

The taxi rank is located next to the exit of the passenger terminal. There is a fixed rate to the city center: €22 on weekdays, €24 on weekends, and €25.30 at night. Luggage is an additional fee: €1 per piece.

Bus

Vespucci Airport is well connected to Santa Maria Novella train station in Florence. It can be reached in just 20 minutes by the Volainbus bus line of the Sita/Ataf company. The express bus departs every half hour from 6 am to 11:30 pm (from the city – from 5:30 am to 11 pm) and takes passengers to the square in front of the station. The fare is €6. Tickets can be bought at the ticket office at the airport or from the driver.

Pisa International Airport

- Piazzale D'Ascanio, 56121 Pisa PI
- +39050849111

You might be arriving via Pisa Airport. Here, you have two options: 1. Buy the second book in the series, or the complete edition, and start by exploring Pisa, then travel to Florence. 2. Head directly to Florence.

How do I get from Pisa Airport to Florence?
You have three transfer options from Pisa Airport to Florence: taxi, bus, or train. Taking an airport taxi or private transfer is your quickest transfer option, with a journey time of one hour and 20 minutes and a cost of around €170. The Sky Bus Lines Caronna bus will take around one hour 30 minutes to reach Florence but will cost just €15. Taking the train from Pisa Airport to Florence is your cheapest transfer option, with a cost of €14 and a journey time of one hour and 30 minutes.

How much is a taxi from Pisa Airport to Florence?
The local taxi drivers don't offer an official set fare for the journey from Pisa Airport to Florence. However, the average fare they will offer for up to four people is €170.

If you'd prefer the peace of mind that comes with a fixed fare, I suggest booking your airport transfers in advance with Welcome Pickups.

Where do I find a taxi at Pisa Airport?
The taxi rank is located directly outside the Arrivals Hall of the main Terminal Building at Pisa Airport.

Convenience
If you're looking for a completely private and direct way to get from Pisa Airport to Florence and your hotel, a Pisa Airport taxi is your best bet. Your journey time will be just one hour and 20 minutes, and your driver will drop you off at the hotel door, safe and sound.

How do I get the bus from Pisa Airport to Florence?

Sky Bus Lines Caronna runs a Pisa Airport to Florence bus daily. The journey time is around one hour and 30 minutes.

How much is the bus from Pisa Airport to Florence?

The cost of a daytime ticket is €15, and the cost of a nighttime ticket is €25. You can purchase tickets online in advance or from the bus driver.

Where do I find the bus at Pisa Airport?

As you step out of the main Terminal Building, you will see the bus stops in front of you. The Sky Bus Lines Caronna bus is bright orange.

Convenience

Taking the bus is much cheaper but not the best option. The bus will arrive at Vespucci Airport, from which you will need to travel to the city and then to your hotel.

Train

I think the train option isn't worth considering. There is no direct train from Pisa Airport to Florence, and you will have to make transfers, which is very inconvenient with luggage.

<u>Florence Santa Maria Novella (train station)</u>

- Piazza della Stazione, 50123 Firenze FI
- Trenitalia.com

From this station, you will head to the next stop on our journey: Pistoia. The ticket costs €5 on the carrier's website, and the travel time is about half an hour. You can also buy the ticket at the station, either at the ticket counter or from a machine. The ticket will be valid for one day. To activate it, you will need to validate it before boarding. You don't need to validate your electronic ticket; just show the QR code from the mail or the ticket code from the SMS to the conductor.

Pistoia (train station)

- Piazza Dante Alighieri, 51100 Pistoia PT

Car rental

Book your car online right after you buy your tickets. This will save you some money.
To rent a car in Italy, you will need three documents:
- Passport
- Bank card
- Driver's license

As a rule, you must be at least 25 years old.
If your name in the documents is translated from your native language into English, make sure the spelling is the same.
Some companies accept only credit cards and not debit cards. If you're allowed to use a debit card, you might have to pay an increased deposit. Also, I recommend taking out full insurance for the duration of the rental.

Taxi

You can order a taxi through the app or find one at special parking lots. These lots are typically near railway stations, metros, shopping centers, and airports. There is a €5 boarding fee and then an additional fee of €1.35 every 1 kilometer.

Conclusion

The Guide and I into that hidden road
Now entered, to return to the bright world;
And without care of having any rest

We mounted up, he first and I the second,
Till I beheld through a round aperture
Some of the beauteous things that Heaven doth bear;
Thence we came forth to rebehold the stars.

Inferno: Canto XXXIV, 133-139.

Here, our journey through the city of Dante, Petrarch, Boccaccio, and Michelangelo comes to an end. I hope you felt their unseen presence in the squares, along the riverbanks, on the bridges, and in the winding streets. If you did, it means I have done my job well, and my guide has helped you, my dear reader, discover the Florence that cannot be revisited, the one that is most precious and that, for this reason, remains forever in the hearts of everyone who has ever seen Brunelleschi's dome rising above terracotta roofs.

If your journey through Tuscany is just beginning here, I invite you to explore the second part of my Tuscan duology: a detailed guide to the major "cities of art" in this wonderful region. These cities are Lucca, Pisa, San Gimignano, Siena, and Arezzo. I dare to believe that you will enjoy your travels through these cities just as much as you enjoyed your long-awaited visit to Florence.

I do not say goodbye but, rather, until we meet again in Tuscany.

Sincerely yours,

George Esperidis.

Made in the USA
Las Vegas, NV
22 November 2024

12404692R00107